Loughrigg
Tales of a small mountain

Eileen Jones

Eileen Jones

Loughrigg: Tales of a small mountain

Copyright Eileen Jones, 2024

Eileen Jones has asserted the right under the Copyright, Designs, and Patent Act, 1988, to be identified as Author of this work.

Cover design by Lucy Frontani
Cover photo by the author
Set in Garamond by Carnegie Book Production
Printed in the UK by Short Run Press.

First published by Gritstone Publishing Co-operative Ltd.

Gritstone Publishing Co-operative Ltd
Birchcliffe Centre
Hebden Bridge
West Yorkshire, HX7 8DG

ISBN 978-1-913625-12-2

CONTENTS

Grasmere

Rydal Water

Rydal

A591

Loughrigg Fell

335m

Loughrigg Tarn

Lily Tarn

Todd Crag

Skelwith Bridge

A593

AMBLESIDE

Windermere

0 SCALE 1

MILES

Jim Tyson

ACKNOWLEDGEMENTS

Throughout this book the 'tales' of this small mountain are stories told to me by many people, and I'm very grateful to all who shared words, pictures, and memories, especially the 'folks who live on the hill' who opened their homes and hearts to me. Particular thanks to Ben Abdelnoor who knows how to run up and down Loughrigg far better than most, and has been recording his own love of the fell for many years. Pete Martin is another who knows Loughrigg intimately and was kind enough to share his expertise. Another with a passion for the hill is Jane Renouf who has walked it daily, whenever possible, since 1975. More pertinently, Jane gave me access to the fantastic resource of the Ambleside Oral History archive, which has been part of her life's work. The Heaton Cooper family feature prominently, deservedly so, and I'm very grateful to Becky Heaton Cooper and Julian Cooper for all their help.

Jim Tyson, runner and cartoonist, created the fabulous frontispiece map, and Martin Bagness gave me permission to use his specialist orienteering map of Loughrigg. Photos came from Steve Ashworth, Chris Routledge, Liz Wakelin, Julie Coldwell and many others.

ACKNOWLEDGEMENTS

To my editor Sheila Seacroft, and others who read various chapters, my thanks for your keen eyes. And thanks to Penny Bradshaw whom I asked for a few words and she sent me a whole chapter, which is wonderful.

I borrowed an idea from my Gritstone colleague Chris Goddard whose guidebooks covering the entire England Coast Path include a song for every section of the route, so there's a soundtrack here for each chapter.

Thanks, of course, to all my colleagues at Gritstone Publishing for their enthusiastic support, and to Lucy Frontani at Carnegie Book Production for being so calm and reassuring.

Since I started work on this project, my life has changed immensely as I now have a grandson, and I want to dedicate this book to Jacques Peter Burnip in the hope that he will learn to love Loughrigg as much as I do.

CHAPTER ONE

MY MOUNTAIN

Panorama. Let's start south-easterly with Windermere, shimmering away to the horizon, Wray castle on the north-western shore, and then Esthwaite Water, Black Fell hiding a view of Coniston Water, in the foreground Elterwater and its village and quarries and then the Coniston fells: the Old Man, a peep of Brim Fell, mighty Wetherlam, across the top of Wrynose to Pike o' Blisco. The serrated edge of the Crinkle Crags, maybe just a hint of Scafell (though not the Pike), the Langdale Pikes themselves with Silver How in the foreground. Swinging north-west where Ullscarf is in the far distance, and a segment of Grasmere just below, Helm Crag dominating the view, before a tiny end of Thirlmere above Dunmail Raise. Seat Sandal and Dollywaggon, and then the full glory of the Fairfield Horseshoe, all eight summits visible from here, across to Red Screes, the distant Kentmere fells and then – home. There's where I've run from, in a cluster of white painted houses just north of Ambleside.

Where others count sheep when they can't sleep, this is my litany, a virtual 360-degree recital of the view from the top of Loughrigg, my mountain. For years, before I came to

1

live in Cumbria, the routine was more of a movie in my mind, a slow-motion reel in which I'd be running up and over the many little paths that lead mesmerisingly around and over the broad hulk of this miniature mountain. I was several years into the life of my new home when it dawned on me that I was, literally, living the dream.

Over the past 13 years I've been up Loughrigg about once a week, probably more than 600 ascents. Mostly running, occasionally walking, I've been up here with small children and small dogs, mountain goats and absolute beginners, though usually solo. I've slept up here, served afternoon tea to passers-by, spent a day up here hula-hooping, listened to a cellist playing Popper's *Gavotte,* and watched as a Border Television reporter filmed Christopher Wordsworth Andrew reading *The world is too much with us,* written by his great great great great grandfather. More of which, later.

Dorothy Wordsworth, the sister of his great great great great grandfather, came up here a lot, too, though peak-bagging wasn't a thing back then, and people walked up and over mountains as part of a daily routine. Dorothy wrote about Loughrigg regularly in her Journal, a wonderful diary of life at Dove Cottage in Grasmere where she and William lived from 1800-1803. And then, for the rest of her life till she died in 1855, she lived with William and his wife Mary even closer to the fell, at the glorious Rydal Mount. They might even have been the first people to climb to the summit of Loughrigg, rather than merely walk along its flanks on the way to Ambleside. In kit we would find preposterous; no gore-tex, no waterproof boots.

But given that it rains rather a lot in the Lake District, I've experienced a surprising number of clear, bright views, though there have been occasions when it was necessary to crawl on hands and knees to touch the summit column, such was the strength of the wind. I've sunbathed at the top, kicked steps in the snow to get there, waded through bogs on the way up, always full of delight.

This isn't about breaking records, of course. Retired doctor Mike Troup, whom we shall meet later, goes up Loughrigg far more often, precisely 113 times in 2023, and that will probably mean more actual summit ascents because, as he says, "I always go to the top at least once per run". Lindsay Buck goes up a Lakeland mountain several times a week, and not just any old fell but the big daddy of them all, Scafell Pike. Lindsay is known as the Wasdale Womble as she collects litter along the way and often posts photos of her day's haul on Facebook.

Lindsay (who, incidentally, won a team gold medal in the over-60 category in the 2023 World Mountain Running Championships in Portugal) retired in 2011 and that's when she started her regular ascents. "I'm not an obsessive; I don't go up every day." This, from the woman who, when we spoke in the summer of 2023, was on 157 ascents so far that year. Her friend Mick Pearce – another Womble – was on 68. "It's just getting to know a mountain in all seasons and guises which adds to appeal."

Small in stature, but massive in bulk, Loughrigg (pronounced Luffrigg) is a sprawling two-mile long misshapen wedge of rough country rising between the valleys of the rivers Brathay and Rothay on the outskirts of Ambleside. The name means 'ridge of the lough (lake)'. Her height (for I see her as female) is 1101ft (335m), so only *just* a mountain by English standards. Of the 214 peaks listed by Alfred Wainwright in his seven *Pictorial Guides to the Lakeland Fells*, Loughrigg scrapes in at number 211. Only Black Fell, Holme Fell and Castle Crag are lower. But Wainwright loved this one, "having a bulk out of all proportion to its modest altitude... no ascent is more repaying for the small labour involved in visiting its many cairns."

Sprawling and confusing, not only in mist but at any point when concentration is lost. Several times I've been convinced that pixies have moved Lily Tarn, and experienced orienteers, as we shall see, will agree that the footpath network has a certain complexity. A. Harry Griffin, who wrote many books about the Lakes, and knew the area very well indeed, wrote:

> Years ago I would be up betimes on Boxing Day to enjoy the challenge of rock, ice or snow but nowadays there's the increasing temptation of a later start and the gentler delights of something like Loughrigg Fell. You could describe Loughrigg, with its little crags, tarns, woodland and sprinkling of summits, as Lakeland in miniature ... . Since Loughrigg is mostly the resort of unambitious walkers or first time visitors it is odd that most of the multitude of paths seem to lead everywhere except to the summit which must have eluded many. I remember once, in thick cloud and heavy

rain, failing to find it – defeat on a familiar thousand-footer. (*A Lakeland Mountain Diary: From 40 Years in the Guardian Country Diary*)

Loughrigg is accessible, easily reached and easily ascended and yet with a real sense of mountaineering if you choose to make the final scramble rather than going round the walkers' way. She's often the first fell climbed, or saved till last, by those ticking off all the summits, but within her spread lies possibly more variety and complexity of landscape and terrain in a small space than anywhere else in the Lake District. The fell has a peculiar and surprising history, having hosted riflemen and golfers along with quarry-workers and sheep farmers.

Around her base can be found a variety of lake and woodland wildlife, while on her slopes are rocks and bogs, a contorted mixture of little pools along with two exquisitely beautiful tarns. It's the texture of the surface, the variety of rock and vegetation, that fascinates the natural historian, and while there's nothing special in terms of rare nesting and over-wintering birds, there's a delightful selection of 'low level' species: wheatears and chiff-chaffs, stonechats and meadow pipits, though the yellowhammers have gone and the skylarks no longer breed here. I'll be introducing you to an expert whose knowledge of the natural history of this little mountain is unsurpassed.

So it's not hard to love Loughrigg. I was once engaged, briefly, to a man who asked what I'd like for my birthday, and I said: "A day out in the Lakes, please." He had a car, and I didn't. We parked by Miller Bridge, and he sat in the car and read the Sunday papers while I went for a walk part way up Loughrigg (only part way, note). I returned the engagement ring at the end of that day.

I'd started climbing the Wainwrights several years before that, without knowing at the time that there was a man called Wainwright or that he wrote guidebooks. We were on a youth hostelling holiday to the Lakes after our 'O' Levels, six of us, all equally clueless. On the first day we walked four miles along the main road from Ambleside to Grasmere, oblivious of safer and more delightful alternatives under Loughrigg or along the Coffin Trail. We had maps, but no one really knew what to do with them, which is why we walked on the second day all the way up the A591 from Grasmere to Wythburn church, and then climbed Helvellyn. At the top, aware that the next hostel was 'down there' at Glenridding, we had a collective fit of the vapours at the sight of Striding Edge, but somehow managed to scramble down Swirral in our smooth-soled 'Spanish' fell boots and carrying enormous framed canvas rucksacks.

The rest of the holiday involved local buses and very little walking but in spite of the terror, I was hooked. I'd never seen anything so magnificent or experienced anything so exhilarating. Family holidays until then had been a week at a guest house in Fleetwood or St Annes; I told mum and dad about the Lakes, obsessing relentlessly, until they too went up to have a look, and also fell in love. They say it changed their lives. They were the ones who first bought decent boots and maps and Wainwright guides; and for the next 42 years most of MY holidays were spent in the Lakes.

The first ascent of Loughrigg was in the early 1970s with a friend from journalism college, Mary, with whom I started to tick off other Wainwrights. When I started running in the 1980s it became possible to knock off eight or nine summits, not in a day but in a few hours, though it wasn't until much later, when we started walking with our own children, that I realised I'd done well over half of the list. The final one, Brock Crags, was achieved in June 2010, just 42 years after the start of the adventure. When, subsequently, I helped Paul Tierney on his record-breaking run, I was proud to be photographed alongside the man who'd completed them all in just over six days.

During those years there were several walks over, on and around Loughrigg, though she was abandoned as the quest intensified. Living in Yorkshire, I'd drive to the Lakes for a day just to bag something remote in the northern or western fells, or use the Achille Ratti climbing club hut in Langdale as a base. Family holidays meant ensuring that the boys, Michael and David, got their own lists under way, sometimes joyously on 'proper' mountains like Blisco and the Old Man, less enthusiastically on others. Yes, we did drag them on the swampy trudge from Bleaberry Fell to High Seat which Wainwright recommends "only as a penance for sins"; they've been very forgiving in return.

It was when I moved to Ambleside, a few months after the ascent of Brock Crags, that Loughrigg became the obvious fell to climb. I had no need to chase other targets, it was so convenient, just a five-minute jog from home to the start of the climb near Miller Bridge. And expedient, too. I love being in the hills, on the tops, but longer walks and runs were becoming difficult. After 40 years of hurtling downhill, the knees are in remarkably good condition, but my feet are no longer fit for purpose. One is riddled with arthritis and unstable, the other, poor thing, is a deformed mess, a neuroma or two behind toes which bend and twist in all the wrong directions. Wearing shoes of any kind for more than a couple of hours is no longer easy, but (so far) I can get up and down Loughrigg in less time than that.

The surgeon to whom I was referred advised against operating. While I could still run 5k, and climb a small mountain once a week, he thought it preferable to keep moving. The operation, he said, would be complex and might be only partially successful, and I would have at least six months out of action. It hurts, but all I have to do is keep moving and breathing and putting one foot in front of the other, though ever more slowly.

There's a lot of running happens on and over Loughrigg, deserving of a chapter of its own. These days I volunteer to staff the registration desk in Rothay Park on the evening of the April fell race, but I've taken part a few times. On one occasion I would have been last, but for an American partially-sighted road runner who was tackling the course with a guide on either side. The last time I took part, I was third from the back, and with a real sense of achievement coupled with the knowledge that I could never do better than this (57 minutes, to the top and back) I offered to volunteer the following year.

By the end of 2023 it was taking me around 53 minutes to reach the summit of Loughrigg from home, but during the pandemic lockdown I managed to get that time down to 38 minutes. There was nothing else to do when all my work dried up, and there was no parkrun weekly motivation, so when I heard that a younger woman in the village was walking up very quickly, I rose to her challenge. For several weeks we outpaced one another, until she gracefully accepted defeat. Well, in truth, she moved to the North Lakes. I would run up, but then walk down; we were urged at the time by the local mountain rescue team to avoid the high fells as their ability to rescue us would be tricky in full PPE kit, and as several members of the team live in my street, I felt doubly obliged to be law-abiding. Accidents would be much more likely on the descent, I reckoned (and there were some very dark times when I thought that dying on a fellside would be preferable to the torture of lockdown isolation).

But there was one particularly joyous ascent during those bleak days. My birthday is in April, and I was determined to celebrate somehow on my favourite mountain, and managed to meet, 'accidentally on purpose', a friend who would come with me. As we neared the summit, I noticed a balloon tied to a stone near the base of the trig column. Going closer, I realised it was also tied to a parcel and a card bearing my name. The parcel contained a slice of chocolate brownie, a gift from some lovely young neighbours who knew I'd be going up there that day. The best-ever birthday cake.

Lockdown did at least force us all to get outside more and, if you recall, the first year of the pandemic, 2020, had a particularly beautiful and mild spring. I would walk all over and around the hill for longer than when I had to rush back for work, sometimes with a socially-distanced friend. How odd it seems now that we were ordered to 'stay home' indoors, just venturing outside once a day for exercise, when subsequently it became apparent that the coronavirus was much less likely to be spread outdoors. That 'once a day' here, surrounded by empty hills, could be for as long as we liked. And so I followed paths not previously taken, headed to many subsidiary summits to check out a different view, and tried to improve my navigational skills.

Orienteering had never been an end in itself, in the days when I did a lot of fell-running. I learned how to navigate, obviously, but not the esoteric lexicon of what I saw as a more complex and serious occupation. Was a boulder the same as an outcrop or a spur? But during the spring of 2020, two separate orienteering challenges were set on Loughrigg, with control points that were left in place for some months. One was established by John Gomersall of Ambleside AC whose course was challenging, but manageable, and took us to some delightful off-piste corners of my mountain. The other was, frankly, a brute. It was set by Martin 'Bilbo' Bagness, a British Orienteering competitor and twice British champion. He has since helped organise an event on Loughrigg where paths were removed from the event map, on the grounds that it is not the most technically challenging area in the Lake District, mostly because it is open, rather than forest, which means you can see a lot further. You can spot a hill 400 metres away and run to it. We'll meet Martin again later.

Martin's challenge was posted online, and I set off emboldened by my (relative) success on John's course. I started at my beloved and familiar Lily Tarn, and after an hour and a half I gave up, having failed to find the first checkpoint. After that, I enlisted the help of an experienced orienteer and general mountain-wise woman, Ruth Halsey, who would walk behind me, gently offering hints as I struggled to interpret Martin's map. How folk manage to run AND do this is beyond me.

John Gomersall says, simply, that he set up his course "to give people things to do. We couldn't go out in a group, we were isolated. It brought people together in a different sort of way, as they uploaded their times onto the website. It helped keep a sense of community while we couldn't be together."

The Ambleside AC club organises an orienteering race annually on and around Loughrigg, a 'score' event with marked points to be visited within an hour. For his lockdown challenge John used an OS map, "worked out some places" and went out with some little wooden pegs as markers, and then told everybody it was there. He started at a point on the tarmac track above the beginning of the climb from the Ambleside direction. It's something he was used to doing, with a background in orienteering, as well as mountaineering and fell running, and as a former outdoor education worker.

John trained as a primary school teacher in Liverpool, then took a job at an outdoor centre in Wales. That's where he married Jane, also a teacher, but without the Welsh language she couldn't get a job in a school in Wales so they moved to Manchester. John then worked in children's homes and as a special needs teacher, doing outdoor education with children and young people. He came to fell running through mountaineering, and maintains that he was never a fast runner, always a plodder, and he joined Ambleside AC when he took early retirement to the Lakes. "Loughrigg is a great playground for runners. It has such variety; you can run over it or around it, you can put in two or three climbs." John will also turn up in a later chapter.

Some of my friends here in Ambleside enjoyed the relative peace of lockdown, the solitude of walks and runs on the hill, but I like people, and I like talking to strangers, especially on my mountain. So I was very glad indeed when the visitors came back. There's often someone else at the top, and I'll ask which way they've come up, and are they on holiday, and if so, from where, which leads inevitably to my introducing parkrun into the conversation. "You're from Sheffield! Ah, I loved Endcliffe parkrun." Or: "Oh Wigan, you have that lovely parkrun at Haigh Hall!" Sometimes the conversation develops further to include my authorship of two parkrun books. On one famous occasion, when I'd chatted to another runner for some time, my friends in Fred's Bookshop in the village subsequently posted on Twitter:

A man came into the shop. He said: "I've just met a woman..." We said: Congratulations! He said: "... on Loughrigg" and we said, you must have come in for this, then.

As a result of those books I was invited to speak at the Swindon Festival of Literature, whose director, Matt Holland introduced me as "the only person who can talk for longer about parkrun than I can". After the event a woman in the audience came to say hello. "You won't remember me, but we met on the summit of Loughrigg last autumn." But I did remember, because she and her husband were on the volunteer team at Lydiard parkrun.

But not all conversations led in that direction. I was once followed to the summit by a man from Wigan who was playing a song on his phone as he walked. He explained that it was the favourite song of his partner who had terminal cancer, and though it made him cry to hear it, he also felt as though she was there walking with him. He was very frank, talked openly about her, showed me photos of her on his phone, all rather matter-of-factly. And then we went our separate ways, only I was the one crying all the way down.

There will be many other stories to follow, most of them joyful. The people I've met on the hill, the folk who live on the hill, the lads and lasses who race over it, the artists who've painted it and the poets who've hailed it, the birds and the beasts, will all be here in subsequent chapters. This doesn't aim to be a precise, definitive or encyclopaedic guide to Loughrigg. It's the stories of people who fell in love with her, the tales of a small mountain. And be sure to say hello if ever we meet on the summit, or part of the way up. Unlike Wainwright, I'm always happy to stop for a chat.

Loughrigg by Kerry Darbishire
The lough of summer skies –
Lily tarn – her eye on wild geese,
autumn's grey beard where at the death
of a year I clung to icy waves up and all the way,
my mother yards ahead at the rigg
where we anchored to sluice the ropes
around our hearts. A fell, full sail, our ship
of sundew, fern and basking vipers,
the broken route we took daily
from here to there.

First published: Black Bough Poetry, Spring Collection 2023.

Soundtrack: Stairway to Heaven, Led Zeppelin

CHAPTER TWO

THE LIE OF THE LAND

Loughrigg is only a little mountain. If indeed it's a mountain at all. Technically, both geologists and the Oxford English Dictionary maintain that a mountain is at least 2,000 feet (or 610 metres) high. Ask a child to draw a mountain, and the result might be a triangular silhouette (maybe inspired by a piece of Toblerone), something like Great Gable. Which definitely qualifies at 2949 feet (899 m). But what about the distinctive and instantly recognisable outline of Helm Crag, which rises a mere 1,329 feet (405 metres) above the village of Grasmere? And what you call a mountain depends on your location. Something you call a mountain in the UK wouldn't necessarily be looked on as a mountain in the Himalaya.

The top of Loughrigg, just 335m/1100ft, looks and feels like a mountain, with its particularly imposing trig column surrounded by craggy rocks. Yet it's 1000ft shorter than Mungrisdale Common, a featureless expanse of upland common that peak-baggers struggle to find on a bright and clear day, let alone in mist. And for perspective, if ever you have the misfortune to be travelling along the M62, a scenic but deeply unpleasant and dangerous road, you might note the sign at the motorway's highest point. At Windy Hill near Denshaw (53.62982°N 2.018561°W) you are 1,221 feet (372 m) above sea level, the highest point of any motorway in England. That's 121 feet higher than Loughrigg.

But she's my mountain, if technically just a fell, and a small one at that, and 'fell' is an honourable word. I shall use both, interchangeably. Precision comes from the artist William Heaton Cooper who wrote prosaically, in *The Hills of Lakeland* (Warne, 1938): "Loughrigg is the name given to a stretch of three square miles or so of rough ground, rising to 1100 feet, surrounded by valleys across which the great hills can be seen, as it were, at arm's length and at right angles to their general slope, in fact in their true proportion."

But the landscape in this part of the country resists categorisation. The poetry comes from Ben Abdelnoor who calls this sprawling mass of land "an overground rabbit warren". You'll meet Ben regularly in these pages, but for many years he's walked over the fell, run over it, got lost on it, and lived on it, and knows it pretty well. Loughrigg, geographically, lies in the central part of the Lake District and is on the end of a long ridge that comes down over High Raise towards Ambleside, separated from its neighbours by the depression at Red Bank. Small in height, maybe, but this sprawling mass of hummocks and little valleys and hundreds of tiny tarns, has territory of monumental proportions, criss-crossed by many paths which make it so easy to get lost if you're not concentrating. Just like a rabbit warren.

Loughrigg means 'ridge above the lough (lake)' and she is surrounded by an unusual amount of open water, though this makes the eponymous Loughrigg Tarn a tautology. To the north the River Rothay flows through both Grasmere and Rydal Water bending around the eastern side of the hill, while on the southern flank the River Brathay runs from Elterwater and is also fed by the outfall from Loughrigg Tarn. The two rivers merge at Clappersgate to the south-east, just before flowing into Windermere, and the western boundary is formed by Red Bank, a road which climbs to 535 ft, on the ridge to Silver How. Unnamed becks fall north and south into Grasmere and Elterwater.

There are two subsidiary ridges on its eastern flank. Lanty Scar provides the obvious line of ascent from Rydal, while the spur rising over Todd Crag leads up from Clappersgate. There are many small areas of woodland on the lower slopes, giving way to a wide expanse of bracken-clad knolls and small tarns on the top. The summit is on the western side of the plateau, but there are also many lower tops which confuse visitors. At the top there's a superb vista to the south all along the length of Windermere, and magnificent mountain scenery in every other direction.

There's a girdle of lakes; from the summit you can see, as well as Windermere, stretches of Elterwater, Esthwaite Water, Grasmere, and a tiny corner of Thirlmere, though the nearest, Rydal Water, is hidden from sight at this point.

And it's a favourite top because it is easily accessible, while being satisfyingly challenging, surrounded by roads on all sides. The holiday-favourite destinations of Ambleside, Grasmere, Skelwith Bridge and Elterwater are all within reach, and there's a big car park just off the main A591 at White Moss Common to bring the hill close to the laziest of walkers. Along this stretch, visible in places from the main road, is the high level path known as Loughrigg Terrace which offers wonderful lake and mountain views, and in spring is a mass of bluebells above and below. At the eastern end of the terrace are the Rydal caves, the largest of which penetrates around 150ft into the hillside. In fact, as Wainwright points out, there's shelter enough here for the entire population of Ambleside, though many of them would be standing in water.

The caves are the result of quarrying for slate in the 19th century, and the largest is a remarkable cathedral-like cavern, the far walls touched with shades of russet and gold and blue. Access is via an easy scramble at the side, or stepping stones across a shallow pool (full of tiny fish). Swallows used to nest in here. We sang carols in here one Christmas, several hundred people who had walked with lanterns and headtorches in the darkness, to find every crevice in the cave lit with tealights, and a fire burning in the centre. Brass bands have played here, and a flute orchestra, and the instrumental group Ananda from the Sri Chinmoy centre gave a concert here some years ago. Sri Chinmoy was a spiritual teacher who guided many students on the path of meditation and spirituality, and taught the philosophy of self-transcendence. This would have been a particularly apposite location. But today the Instagram generation have brought it too much popularity, and visitors come here just to be photographed, rather than as part of a walk to the heights. Or to play a tune or two.

Most of Loughrigg is owned by the Earl of Lonsdale's Lowther Estate, apart from the land either side of the main bridleway from Miller Bridge to the fell gate. It includes Lily Tarn, though Loughrigg Tarn is owned by the National Trust. Lowther also own common land around Grasmere and Elterwater. Farmers using Loughrigg don't lease the grazing, but they have grazing rights which are permanently attached to their farms, which are registered on the Commons Register at Carlisle.

The Lowther dynasty was founded some 850 years ago, in that top corner of Cumbria that's seen three principal dwellings come and go since the first settlement. Today the Estate is presided over by the ruined Lowther Castle, a Gothic building completed in 1812, deroofed in 1957 and, today, a thriving visitor attraction. Other areas in the Lake District were added, and while the Estate has grown and fluctuated, Lowther has been guided by an abiding will to stay ahead of the times. The benefits of forestry were foreseen during the reign of Edward I; vegetarianism was embraced by Viscount Lonsdale in the late 17th century. Today they have ambitions to promote a more natural environment where biodiversity and species richness increases, and where natural regeneration creates a more diverse range of habitats for birds, insects and mammals. How that rests with traditional sheep farming in the Lakes, and on Loughrigg, we shall see later.

Loughrigg is a walker's and runner's paradise, but not many people realise that there's also a serious, E4 grade rock climb on the Clappersgate side of the fell. It's called Crack in the Woods, 22 metres of it, and there's some seriously impenetrable details here, from the UK Climbing website. It's officially the main buttress of Rothay Bridge Crag and is described as: "A flower growing out of the surrounding choss, if this route were at a better crag, it would be a classic. Climb the obvious concave crackline in the centre of the blank face with sustained powerful jamming moves and deliciously technical footwork. In its current condition, the bottom third of the crack is around 5c, the middle third 6a, and the top third is getting on for 6b." Which some readers will understand.

But now aware of its existence, I was determined to go and have a look, and enlisted the enthusiastic Liz Wakelin, an experienced climber, to join the search party. We set out to find it, at the height of a wet summer, so that our adventure turned into desperate manoeuvres in a rainforest before we found ourselves safely back at the stone stile by the bridleway. There were paths, we're sure, but this area was devastated by Storm Arwen and we had to climb over as many uprooted trees as we did moss-covered boulders. When I last checked the climbing website, only 23 users had logged an ascent, with a further 12 having it on their wish list.

What today's ramblers might also be unaware of are the remains of both a rifle shooting range and a golf course on Loughrigg. The rifle range – in fact, there's evidence of more than one – was used for target practice from the 19th century onwards, when volunteers were called up for service. When in 1859 the Second Italian War of Independence broke out between France and the Austrian Empire, there was concern that Britain might be drawn into a wider European conflict. Public opinion favoured the use of volunteers to fill the home defence gap and, despite reservations on the part of the military, the Secretary of State for War authorised the raising of Rifle Volunteer Corps. The response was astonishing. More than 180,000 men volunteered in the months following the announcement.

For this detail and much more about the ranges I'm indebted to Paul Burke for providing the report on the outcome of a survey of abandoned rifle ranges within the area of what is now the Lake District National Park, carried out by a group from the Lake District Archaeology Volunteer Network. *(Great Grandad's Army, Rifle Ranges of the Lake District, Jeremy Rowan Robinson et al. 2016.)*

The report explains, and I'm going to quote a significant chunk here because you don't want any errors where firing ranges are concerned:

> Above Ambleside on the lower slopes of Loughrigg are the remains of three rifle ranges. The first was a long range of 800 yards running south-east to north-west across access land and then through the field alongside Deer Hows Wood to the target at NY 36047 04840 above the footpath up Fox Ghyll. The second was a short range of 300 yards running south west from a point near to the old Ambleside Golf

Club house with the target at NY 36041 04314. Both ranges
first appear on the Westmorland XXVI.SW 6" OS sheet,
revised 1897. There is nothing to be seen of the long range
target. It was set on a natural platform above the footpath
up Fox Ghyll. A search with the metal detector revealed
Martini Henry and Lee Enfield or Lee Metford .303 bullets.
Signals suggested a spread of spent bullets all around the
target position. The firing positions up to 300 yards from the
target would have been located in what is now a field and
was formerly part of a golf course so it is unlikely there is
anything to be seen. Nothing obvious was observable looking
down from the target position. The 400 yard firing position
would have been located just north of the bridleway from
Ambleside to Langdale but there have been changes in the
terrain following the construction of the Ambleside Golf
Club house and, again, there was nothing obvious to be seen.
There was no constructed firing position at 500 yards and
the grid reference from the 6" OS sheet indicated that it was
probably positioned on or near a rocky knoll. We suspect that
the remaining firing positions up to 800 yards also made use
of natural features.... . Both ranges were discontinued with
the construction of the Ambleside Golf Course which opened
in 1903.

The range near to what is Pine Rigg today was probably
constructed sometime between 1879, when the Martini Henry
rifle first became available to Volunteers, and 1903 when the
range was replaced by the golf course and would have been
used by the Ambleside Company of the 2nd (Westmorland)

Volunteer Battalion of the Border Regiment, the report says. But the golf course was requisitioned for rifle target practice in both the First and Second World Wars.

Yes, golf course. The Ambleside and District Golf Club at Loughrigg was founded in 1903 and was used until 1950. The *Lakes Herald* wrote at the time: "It is somewhat satisfactory to know that the geographical surroundings of the valley are not entirely hostile to golfers." (https://www. golfsmissinglinks.co.uk)

The links were laid out on land leased from Brow Head Farm with the agreement of the tenant, Anthony Chapman. The nine-hole course was designed by the Lytham and St Annes professional, a Mr Lowe, "and a suitable pavilion erected. It is calculated to drag people up into the best possible air and whilst they are pursuing the game they can at the same time enjoy to the full the extensive panorama which Nature has provided," said the *Lakes Herald*.

From the same archive, it was noted that Joseph Pye, professional at Ambleside, formerly of St Annes, collapsed and died after driving off from the seventh tee. It was reported that "While playing round in a Foursome he suddenly complained of feeling out of sorts. His three companions went on leaving him to rest on the seventh tee but on again going round the course they found him, as they had left him, huddled up on the seventh tee." He was 27 years old. A memorial tablet was subsequently placed on the wall in Brathay church by the members of the Ambleside Golf Club and the Brathay church choir. It's still there, go and see.

The Ambleside Oral History archive holds a recorded interview (1997, reproduced here with permission) with Trevor Woodburn who used to play golf there. He took up golf after leaving 'the forces' around 1947, encouraged by a local retired fishmonger Harry Stubbs.

> It (the golf club) was there before the war, yes. What Harry did was cultivate all the younger ones, myself, Harry Shuttleworth, Jack Little, Roland Stephenson, Core Stephenson, Les Stephenson and people like Betty Faulkner, Muriel Barton, we were all about of an age at that time, we would all be in our early 20's and we all became very interested in taking up golf. Harry put his money into it and tarred the road up towards the golf course, and he also was the instrumental in taking the services of a professional golfer and green keeper and he put all the new greens in. This went on for a number of years and I think we all became fairly proficient golfers at that time, because we all had to work and you know times were a bit difficult at the time but it was lovely to be able to go up from Ambleside, up onto Loughrigg and put in a round of golf. Also the professional at the time was a chap by the name of Harold Anderson, and he gave us all tuition, and he helped us no end.

The golf club closed, the club house was converted to a home, and in 1963 it was bought by four friends who loved it, who loved Loughrigg, and whose story is in another chapter. Loughrigg, it seems, is easy to love, and certainly Alfred Wainwright fell for her charms. In *A Pictorial Guide to the Lakeland Fells: Book Three, The Central Fells* he devotes 16 pages to this tiddler, which comes in at number 211 in his collection of 214 Lakeland summits. He says, and I make no apologies for quoting at length, for AW was writing a love letter to my mountain:

> Of the lesser heights of Lakeland, Loughrigg Fell is pre-eminent. It has no pretensions to mountain form, being a sprawling ill-shaped wedge of rough country rising between the park-like valleys of Brathay and Rothay, and having a bulk out of all proportion to its modest altitude; but no ascent is more repaying for the small labour involved in visiting its many cairns, for Loughrigg has delightful grassy paths, a series of pleasant surprises along the traverse of the summits, several charming vistas and magnificent views, fine contrasts of velvety turf, rich bracken and grey rock, a string of little tarns like pearls in a necklace, and a wealth of stately trees on the flanks. It is especially well-endowed with lakes, with four sheets of water, all lovely, touching its lower slopes, and in addition it nurses a large tarn to which it gives its name – and this is a distinction not attained by any other fell. It has also more paths to the square mile than any other fell, great or small, and amongst them is one that far exceeds in popularity any other in the district, one that all visitors know: Loughrigg Terrace… . In brief this fell has a wealth of interests and delights, and for many people who now find pleasure in walking over the greater mountains it served as an introduction and an inspiration. Everybody likes Loughrigg.

> (NB Storm damage and disease has made poorer that 'wealth of stately trees'.)

Wainwright includes six pages of directions to reach the summit, ascents from many different starting points. "When fellwalking, it is better to arrive than to travel hopefully and this is the justification for the inclusion here of six pages... because, although of insignificant altitude, the fell has an extensive and confusing top, the ultimate objective remains hidden on the approach, and the maze of paths needs careful unravelling – besides, failure would be too humiliating!"

It seems pertinent here to talk a little more about Alfred Wainwright. There will be devotees who can skip the next few paragraphs, but there are generations of visitors who now ask, "What's a Wainwright?" They might be the ones who come to climb the fells equipped with little more than a mobile phone and Google Maps; the notion of carrying a paper map, a compass *and* a small hardback book is clearly beyond their ken. But Wainwright changed the concept of fell-walking, for better or worse, introducing new audiences, new adventurers, new readers to a pastime that certainly changed their lives.

His series of seven guidebooks to different areas of the Lakes has been in print almost continuously since it was first published between 1955 and 1966, with well over two million copies sold. It is still regarded by many walkers as the definitive guide to the Cumbrian hills. The books consist entirely of reproductions of Wainwright's manuscripts, hand-produced in pen and ink with no typeset material, with gorgeously detailed maps and drawings; it's likely that no one had produced a book like this, entirely hand-written, since the monks of the Middle Ages.

Between 2005 and 2009, the series was factually revised by the current publishers, Frances Lincoln, to adjust the content to the present-day Lake District. Chris Jesty undertook the revisions, using an imitation of Wainwright's hand lettering to make the alterations look as unobtrusive as possible. The most notable changes are that the covers of the revised books show photographs of the Lake District by Derry Brabbs, rather than the drawings that were on the covers of the originals, and the maps show the main paths in red.

Born in Lancashire, Wainwright – AW as he liked to be called – was an accountant in Blackburn town hall when, at the age of 23 in 1930, he visited the Lake District for the first time. He travelled by bus to Windermere with his cousin and on their arrival, they climbed the 780ft of Orrest Head where, as Wainwright wrote later, 'Orrest Head cast a spell that changed my life'. It was the view from the top that proved to be the turning point.

> It was a moment of magic, a revelation so unexpected that I stood transfixed, unable to believe my eyes. I saw mountain ranges, one after another, the nearer starkly etched, those beyond fading into the blue distance. Rich woodlands, emerald pastures and the shimmering waters of the lake below added to a pageant of loveliness, a glorious panorama that held me enthralled. I had seen landscapes of rural beauty pictured in the local art gallery, but here was no painted canvas; this was real. This was truth. God was in his heaven that day and I a humble worshipper. (*Ex-Fellwanderer*, 1987.)

It was the beginning of a love affair which turned AW eventually and inadvertently into a legend. He moved to live and work in Kendal in 1941 and began to explore the hills and mountains, climbing to many of the summits. In November 1952 he began work on his *Pictorial Guides*, an idea that had been slowly germinating for many years. The first page completed on that first evening was the ascent of Dove Crag from Ambleside.

This was the start of a literary career that occupied the next four decades until his death in January 1991. A non-driver, he always travelled on public transport until the final guidebook when his second wife Betty would drive him to locations. His division of the Lake District into seven distinct geographical areas – Eastern, Far Eastern, Central, Southern, Northern, North Western and Western Fells – was as arbitrary as his selection of 214 summits. Bill Birkett in 1994 published a guide to the *Complete Lakeland Fells* which lists 541 hills within the Lake District National Park boundary which are over 1000ft/304m. In that list Loughrigg comes in at number 506. And of course there are peak-baggers who tick off all the Birketts as well as the Wainwrights, though after completing all the Wainwrights in 2010, a mere 42 years after first climbing Helvellyn, my own fell-wandering was replaced with the Loughrigg obsession.

AW's obsession took up every spare moment of his waking life, and there is so much that his books, originally written for his own personal memory, a souvenir for his old age, have given to others. He made maps accessible for those who hadn't used them before. (Some used to argue that he stopped people from learning how to read a map properly, and that when they went off 'the page' they blamed Wainwright for their own navigational failures. But today, with a cavalier over-reliance on technology in areas with no mobile signal and no re-charging point, a Wainwright guide would be considered a massive additional assistance.)

But as well as being used on the hill, the guidebooks are full of fascinating detail, observation and humour, so they can be read at home after the walk, to bring back memories, or to help imagine the fells for those no longer able to reach the heights. AW last walked on the hills with the broadcaster Eric Robson who was interviewing him for a TV documentary. When he died in 1991, his ashes were scattered on a favourite mountain of his, Haystacks, beside Innominate Tarn, as he had wished.

A living legend, though he would balk at the notion, is Martin Bagness, who really does know Loughrigg better than anyone, in the physical sense. A climber, runner, and orienteering cartographer by profession, who moved to Ambleside nearly 40 years ago to set up a business making maps, he has produced the ultimate orienteering map of the fell. Affectionately known as Bilbo, he knows every single one of its lumps and bumps, and its many tarns. How many? "Well, it depends what you mean by a tarn…?".

Martin produced an orienteering challenge over Loughrigg to keep local runners and wayfinders from going mad during the pandemic lockdown. But unlike the one created by John Gomersall (we will meet him later) Martin's map actually drove some of us mad with despair. After spending 1.5 hours to find just the first checkpoint, I had to enlist a (socially distanced) expert friend to guide me around my own mountain.

Martin says: "For the expert orienteer it's not a really difficult hill because there's no forest or woodland. But unless you are an expert, I suppose it is tricky. In fact, it's one of the toughest fell areas, because it is so spread out. And given its modest height, it's so spread out so that it's set back from everything else. From an orienteering point of view, everything falls away in different directions. There's not an easy structure to it."

But he loves it, of course, and prefers running over Loughrigg to his marginally closer-to-home Wansfell "which is just too vertical. As a runner, Loughrigg has always been the perfect extension to my (non-existent) back garden. It is a fun place to run, because so many of the paths are soft and grassy, with continual twists and turns and ups and downs. Plus there are views in every direction. For an orienteer it's a challenge to weave around the numerous knolls and small tarns on the plateau. Around the sides, small valleys fall away in surprising directions and it is easy to become disorientated. The many paths can also become confusing. Orienteers generally run off-path and for this reason events are usually held in winter and spring due to the killer-bracken."

Martin is author of a number of books including *Mountain Navigation for Runners, Outward Bound*

Orienteering Handbook, and several mountain biking route guides. But he's best known as a cartographer and outstanding competitive orienteer. He was a member of the silver medal-winning relay team at the 1993 World Orienteering Championships and won two competitions at the British championships. He's not been competing much since the early 1990s but is still regarded as a legendary figure in the sport, especially in the Lake District.

In 2020 he was awarded British Orienteering's Bonington Trophy, presented annually for the best contribution to mapping; it reflects his considerable input and support to the sport over many years. The secretary of his club, Warrior Orienteering, said that the award recognised his superb contribution to making orienteering maps for over 35 years. "Martin has sought out and mapped many areas of forest, woodland, open fell and urban areas in the Lake District producing high quality maps in his distinctive readable style, making user friendly maps for everyone to enjoy, from beginners to experts. Martin's recognition for this award is well deserved and we hope he will continue to make maps for many years to come."

Martin adds: "I hope future generations will enjoy a wilder version of Loughrigg than we do today, maybe a controversial point. Different grazing practices, less bracken and sheep-cropped turf, more heather, bilberry and scattered trees together with more diverse fauna."

And finally, a love poem to Loughrigg from Selwyn Wright, writer, runner and race organiser. Selwyn has spent a lifetime running among the hills, and with John Brockbank he was the first runner to complete the 66-mile, 42-peak Bob Graham Round in winter. A competitor for over 40 years, long time organiser of both the Three Shires and Blisco races, running coach and orienteer, he told his life story in the warm and delightful *Just for Fun: Me and Fellrunning*.

Loughrigg

Mostly it's just the little hill next door;
For walk or run, a good session with paths aplenty.
Get your fix for an hour or more
With views to the big hills you'd die for.
Perfect for a race – spring or autumn
In the main. And for the youngsters
It's massive and daunting
Like any playground when you start.
But take it too much for granted
And Loughrigg has an unwelcome habit
It can give you a little nibble;
The bite much worse than the bark.
Most years there's a day
When I'm not quite where I thought
I was – sometimes a good way
From any straight and narrow.
Truth is I love being lost,
And sometimes with Loughrigg
In the dark or in the cloud,
Or just too many paths to choose;
You can enjoy a little adventure
That you didn't quite expect!

Selwyn Wright Jan 2024

Soundtrack: Beethoven Symphony No 6, The Pastoral

CHAPTER THREE

FELLSIDE HABITAT

There's a point at about 200m up the bridlepath from the cattlegrid near Miller Bridge where I'll stop every time, running or walking, solo or with others, to look. Is she home, our Owl? Or he, for until a tawny owl calls, its gender is not easy to recognise. But there she is, today, in that lop-sided heart-shaped hole in an old ash tree, clearly visible if you know where to look, stunningly visible if you've remembered to bring the binoculars. She's our worst-kept secret, for though I won't write down the exact location, I can't help wanting to introduce her to anyone who's coming up or down the hill at that moment. Especially children. Do you want to see an owl, I ask, and minutes later I'm invariably told: "That's made my day".

There's so much to see on Loughrigg if you're not peak bagging, or running to the top, or herding dogs or small children, which rules out rather a lot of human beings here. But there is more of interest here, per hectare, to human beings than anywhere else in the Lake District. That's the subjective but also very likely accurate view of Pete Martin, an amateur natural historian who wanders on and around the fell with the keenest of eyes although, sadly in recent times, not the most well-functioning feet. He's a retired careers adviser who got interested in bird-watching as a child, became "an obsessive gardener" and something of an expert on lichens. He's as modest as the height of his favourite mountain: "I just know what I don't know."

It's the accessibility of Loughrigg that makes it such a regular first Wainwright or final Wainwright or commonest Wainwright, says Pete, "but though lots of people know it, yet they don't know it, because it's almost unfathomable because there's so much there. It's the variety and the complexity of the landscape that make it so special. The history, past use, the sociology, the natural history, all of those elements are wrapped up together to create something that's really fascinating."

To start, the grand overview. A contorted mixture of little crags and excavated pools, whether formed by glaciers or peat cutters. A huge variety of surface textures. All around the fell, a selection of woodland with a variety of trees, all the history of grazing and land ownership in microcosm. All these are features which are common throughout the Lake District. It's what you don't find elsewhere in the Lakes that makes Loughrigg special, says Pete. The curious mixture of rocks that make the landscape, the variety of vegetation because of the different rock types and the acidity of the soil, as well as the variation of drainage and aspect. Which is why you'll find species such as the birds-eye primroses on the 'flushes', the Site of Special Scientific Interest to the south of the main bridleway near Pine Rigg (map ref NY365043). Flushes are areas where water from underground flows out onto the surface to create an area of saturated ground, rather than a well-defined channel.

Here you'll find those primroses, a collection of orchids and sedges, bog asphodel, devils-bit scabious, and my own favourite, in late summer, the grass of Parnassus (*Parnassia palustris*), the flower of Cumberland. "It's not world-staggeringly rare but it's just really, really nice," says Pete. "Then you've got all the juniper bushes which stagger onwards in the dampish zones. Juniper is an amazing shrub that thrives in all sorts of places, it forms a staggering collection of shapes, so there are ones that look like Cypress trees and ones that look like creeping, undulating dinosaurs, or dolphins. Within there is a habitat for birds – especially thrushes – and deer. Juniper, along with its traditional use in making gin, was used to make charcoal and charcoal was used to make gunpowder, so we can perhaps hypothesise that the juniper is there, or stayed there, because of the needs of the gunpowder works at Elterwater."

More about flowers, from a delightful blog called *Cumbria Naturally* where the writer Jan Wiltshire describes a summer visit to Loughrigg, and she's given permission to use this lyrical extract:

> The lambs of Underloughrigg lay fast-asleep in postures of abandonment at 7am. At Fox Ghyll, I emerged from a tunnel of rhododendron and came upon a heaven of bright stars beside the beck: the massed flowers of bog asphodel fade so fast while the seed heads go on and on. There were

orchids and cross-leaved heath, and the white seed-heads
of common cotton-grass. What a show! With open ground
and water there came a lovely botanical mix and a respite
from high bracken which overwhelmed everything else. The
waters of Lily Tarn had drawn back to leave a border of thick
silt and rank vegetation. Now was the time of white water
lilies, flowers of pondweed and water lobelia, and the yellow
hammer sang from his rock redoubt. On Loughrigg Terrace
yellow saxifrage and tormentil would flower through a long
season. Coming off the fell was a zone with bog asphodel
where a water-track drained into Rydal Water. Attracted
by white-flowered sneezewort whose Latin name, *Achillea
ptarmica,* sounds rather like a sneeze, I stepped amongst
tussocks and hidden pockets of water, with white bedstraw,
yellow greater bird's-foot trefoil, and purple thistles pollinated
by bumble bees with white-tails. There were pale moths,
a dark green fritillary sipped nectar from a thistle and an
electric blue damselfly came down on soft rush and closed its
wings. Magic in a patch of ground that merely looked ragged
and overblown a fortnight later.

More trees, too, are surviving higher up on the fell due to
the reduction in sheep grazing, of which more shortly. Says
Pete Martin: "There's some really nice variety of woodland
surrounding Loughrigg, some really old trees, some bits of
old woodland that were very heavily coppiced, like Fishgarths
wood. Bits of footpath that I would call Cherry Tree Barn
field, above Brown Head, the field on the right. But then there
were a few big old trees which came down in Storm Arwen."

Alongside storm damage has been the recent devastating loss of larch and ash trees on the lower slopes of Loughrigg which have succumbed to disease. Phytophthora ramorum is a fungal-like organism that causes the death of a wide range of trees and shrubs, with the greatest impact so far in the Lake District on larch plantations, and they have to be felled. And Chalara fraxinea – commonly known as ash dieback – is now presenting a major challenge to the management of woodlands throughout the Lakes.

Local farmers, and the sustainability group Ambleside Action for a Future, have been planting new trees on the fellside. In spring 2021 they identified the trees planted in cages on Todd Crag ten years previously as in need of maintenance, including removal of bracken. With permission of the owners and tenants of the land, they carried out a survey of the species and condition of each tree in the wooden and metal mesh cages, some 150 in all.

They replaced some that hadn't survived with new trees provided by the Woodland Trust and cut down the bracken around them to aid their survival. They also planted new trees in wooden cages around the main path to Lily Tarn and created four small spinneys outside the cages to provide habitats for birds, mammals and insects. Trees were also planted above Fishgarths wood; at various times they have planted a mix of sessile oak, downy birch, bird cherry, aspen, dog rose, hawthorn, alder, buckthorn, and crab apple.

The AAFAF group also noted a few years ago that the ancient oak woodland of Deer Hows on the foothills of

Loughrigg had been so grazed by deer and sheep that it had no understory, the underlying layer of vegetation in a forest or wooded area, especially the trees and shrubs growing between the forest canopy and the forest floor. Since then, with the permission of the National Trust and the tenant farmer, they have protected more than 100 saplings, primarily oak, and a few hazel, rowan, and birch, with recycled plastic tubes from other plantings, and wooden stakes provided by the Woodland Trust, both in the wood and nearby in a smaller wood and fields by the river Rothay.

Their report notes: "While planting we noticed a marsh tit, which is on the red list (of conservation concern) as well as flycatchers, woodpeckers and buzzards. These and other species need a rich understory to thrive."

Pete Martin explains that Loughrigg is on the 'fly way' through the Lake District "so from a bird point of view it's a fascinating place to be. There's nothing special in terms of rare nesting and over-wintering birds, but there's a delightful selection of 'low level' species: wheatears and chiff-chaffs, stonechats and meadow pipits, though the yellowhammers have gone and the skylarks no longer breed here. It's a stopover point for wheatears; in March the first ones come, in the gully near the summit, that's where they breed and where one would see them first.

"One of the delights is that you get to know things on Loughrigg. You see these things happen every year. The birds disappear and then come back. The stonechats are almost always there but the two harsh winters of 2010 and

2011 wiped them out. And then they started coming back. And there was an order in which they came back, the best territories were re-colonised first. After three years they were back by the route I always went up. And every spring mallards will come into the boggy bit by the rifle range.

"The woods have pied flycatchers, willow warblers, wood warblers sometimes. There used to be woodcock, but I've not seen them roding recently (that's the display, given at dusk and involving birds flying in straight lines above their territories). Then the winter woodcock arrive from Russia, and they hang about in the woods secretively till around April. When our summer ones arrive from Cornwall, or Spain, only the bird ringers know the difference."

The cuckoo always calls, though later than the one on Wansfell across the valley. We note it usually around the last day of April or the first of May, somewhere to the south of Pine Rigg. And our owl? Pete says that a tawny has used that same hole in the winter for at least 15 years, though it won't be the same owl. And it's around here that you might spot a red squirrel, seen more regularly since the campaign to cull the greys started to take effect. When grey squirrels arrive in a red squirrel area, the red squirrel population usually disappears within 15 years. The grey squirrel outcompetes the red for food and space, and carries a disease, the squirrel pox virus. This disease kills the red squirrel but has no known lasting effect on the greys. In circumstances where the presence of squirrel pox is confirmed, the extinction rate of red squirrels can be 20 to 25 times faster than that in pox free areas.

But some conservationists are now saying that culling may actually lead to an increase in grey-squirrel populations because recolonisation occurs rapidly when food and habitat are easily available. And that it's humans who are responsible for encroaching on and destroying massive expanses of woodland, habitats that otherwise could have provided more than enough space for all species to thrive. It's unfair, they say, to scapegoat and kill grey squirrels, who are simply trying to survive. This is a subject for an entire book, someone else's book.

But if you're lucky, you will see a red squirrel, earlier or later in the day. There are voles on Loughrigg too, which means hunting fodder for kestrels. There are roe deer on the hill, the woods are full of them, though red deer are seen only rarely these days. There's a lot of badgers, and closer to the ground adders and slow worms, and even lizards, though you have to be in the right place at the right time on the right day to see them.

In a lovely home video made by Pete Deeley, who lived at the old golf club house at Pine Rigg for 50 years, he makes a season by season tour of the garden, which lies at the 500ft contour. In spring a herd of deer visited for a week, demolishing all they could eat in the garden, but then came the blossoms: berberis and pieris, maple flower and cherry blossom, azalea and hawthorn. Bluebells and foxgloves extend way beyond the garden now, climbing higher up the fellside each year, while closer to the house were hemerocalis, the day lily, and the luscious purple clematis, The President.

By early June birds were filling the garden: nuthatch, great spotted woodpecker, a family of pheasant "though they had to be careful because there was a sparrowhawk about". By summer there were daisies, and flowers on the Korean pine. A lizard sunbathed on the coir doormat, and a slow worm made its way over the gravel. The bright red tropaeoleum flowered among the conifers, the Korean pines started to put out blue cones, and the daisy bush Olearia was in full flower. In July came the Kalmia, white cornus flower, blue speedwell, campanula and potentilla.

In autumn, when there were berries on the rowan trees and the heather was flowering, that's when the red squirrels would cluster around the bird feeders, and a woodmouse and a bank vole were regular visitors "though the stoat tends to grab one or two for his lunch". Colourful kaffir lilies only lasted a day because two splendid antlered deer turned up for a snack. Wind began to strip leaves from the trees, as mushrooms sprouted on the lawn, and a white-mantled blackbird appeared in the garden. "We thought at first it was a coot, but it couldn't be, not at this height." Chaffinch and robins, yellow-hammer and dunnock were all winter visitors to the bird table.

And then we need to talk about sheep. It's hardly wildlife, but sheep play a huge part in the life of Loughrigg, and on the wildlife of the fell. A tricky subject, which changes with political direction, and a subject that rouses passions among those who believe that sheep should be allowed to roam the fells as they have done for many years, and those who see the sheep as a barrier to rewilding.

The effect of sheep on the fell was summed up concisely by farmer Chris Hodgson of Rydal Farm, which lies under Loughrigg, though Chris has sheep – and cattle – that graze on the other side of the valley, in the bowl of the Fairfield Horseshoe. It's called 'Fair Field' for a reason, it was once covered in grass, he pointed out. "Now it looks like the surface of the moon."

Chris was being interviewed on the Tree Amble podcast by Pete Leeson, who has spent 30 years working to restore nature in forests and on farms, and now revisits people he's met along the way. Throughout the series, Pete discovered how land managers are adapting and responding to the nature crisis we all face, while navigating the economic challenges in farming today. "People are at the heart of this podcast, holding the potential to do some incredible things." He talked to farmers, ecologists, and rewilders to find out how communities are building a future together which respects and supports nature.

Chris agrees now that he has changed his own views. "I was a traditionalist. I wasn't into tree planting, it was all about sheep." But having been persuaded to change some of the ways he operates, for example having cattle graze on the fell rather than sheep, he has seen the impact. "I've seen in the last nine years where the sward length has got longer, so as a result there's more insects and as a result of that there's more birds, and so there's more birds of prey, and the peregrines have been back for the first time in 20 years."

Sheep, he recognises, are like lawnmowers, "they will eat

the wild flowers, they will eat the young trees, as well as the grass." One of the events that brought about his conversion was the devastation of Storm Arwen, when many iconic trees that he'd known since his childhood, climbed in his childhood, had gone. That's when he went out and planted replacements.

But nothing is simple. The sheep which were hefted to the fell, that is, had grazed their own areas for generations, wanted to get back in where land had been fenced off, "and they'd be knocking walls down". Now he has fewer sheep but more cattle, which graze on the uplands, though a few cows died from acorn poisoning where new oaks had been planted. "I hate to say this, but for the future, we have to cut down on livestock."

It is an entire book, maybe several volumes, to adequately address the issues here, but Pete Martin helped to summarise the situation. "There has been active encouragement and financial incentives to reduce sheep numbers so as to improve vegetation quality and biodiversity on the fells. It's not simple and straightforward a situation though, and the devil of these things is always in the detail. Different farms will have different individual stories about sheep reduction. Each farm is its own separate business."

There are a number of factors in play where sheep farming is concerned. Agri-subsidies (Common Agriculture Policy pre-Brexit) were once based purely on production. But these were reduced and then removed from stock numbers, so it just didn't pay to have as many sheep as possible. In fact, you got paid just for having the land. Environmental (Stewardship) payments took a larger part of agri-subsidy money over time. For some farmers these involved agreements with Natural England about stocking levels (these might be overall stocking numbers, or stocking numbers at different times of the year, or stocking numbers in different parts of the land to reduce impact on vegetation, be that general vegetation or specific types).

But of course hill sheep farming isn't economic, so a farmer might decide to not do it/do less/ have cattle instead, particularly once subsidy was decoupled from numbers. The pressure of visitor numbers, their dogs, problems caused by gates left open, might mean that a farmer stopped putting sheep on some areas. Or the sheep might decide not to go near tarns where swimmers go with dogs, so the vegetation might recover there. But if the number of sheep is reduced on the common, the hefting system breaks down.

Further clarity, which also highlights the dichotomy, comes from Julia Aglionby. She's Professor in Practice at the University of Cumbria, and specialises in the interface and contested space between agricultural productivity and the provision of public benefits in national parks and protected areas. "Most of my professional work focuses on common land and upland issues. I have worked in this area for over 25 years drawing on my qualifications in the natural sciences, environmental economics and land law." During her career, she's consistently advocated for England's uplands, regularly on BBC Radio 4, regional TV and in the press. A committed supporter of farming communities, she wants to help farmers to run thriving businesses, producing high quality products while also successfully protecting biodiversity, the climate and our cultural heritage.

She acts as the bridge between farmers and others, whether environmental organisations, landowners, water companies or government, to enable the two-way traffic of ideas and information. She told me: "Good farm management, and good support for that, is essential in an area like the Lake District. This is a landscape that needs a lot of management, from the gathering of sheep to the rebuilding of dry-stone walls. Farmers here are stewards of the landscape as well as owning sheep, and the government is not really supportive of fell farming systems.

"The situation is that hill farmers were being offered payment rates far below those paid within the EU, leaving their finances in a precarious state, which is pushing some to increase livestock cultivation rather than restore nature."

The reality of the situation on Loughrigg is seen by Malcolm Murphy who farms at the National Trust property at Tarn Foot, where he has a flock of 500 sheep, mainly Herdwick, bred for wool and meat, and also runs a campsite beside Loughrigg Tarn. He's lived here most of his life, having moved "just along the road" from The Oaks when he was 12. His father and his grandfather both farmed here. But like all who farm on Loughrigg and other fell land, he has fewer sheep now; not so long ago his flock numbered 1000.

Malcolm points out this is not the only change to his

working conditions. In recent years he's noticed changes to weather patterns, with more rain and more easterly winds. His sheep will still lamb in April (from April 5, to be precise, as they went to tup on November 10: "It'll be a chaotic three weeks.") but the campsite won't be fit to open until May. "The campsite goes with the farm tenancy. We used to open in April but it can still be icy or too wet now." When we spoke in January, the tarn was frozen. "But there's nowhere like it, this place. The tarn is one on its own."

So sheep, like squirrels, will no doubt have many books dedicated to them. The Lowther Estate, owning much of Loughrigg, have a distinctive re-wilding policy (https://www. rewildingbritain.org.uk/rewilding-projects/lowther-estate). They are part of the Rewilding Network, the go-to place for projects across Britain to connect, share and make rewilding happen on land – and sea. They have already achieved some impressive results from rewilding of previously farmed lowland areas, including the successful reintroduction of beavers, but a large part of the Lowther estate is made up of uplands typical of the Lake District. The website https://www.replanet.org. uk/ explains: "Most people visit the Lake District and believe that the huge expanses of upland areas are truly wild habitat, but in fact they are heavily disrupted after centuries of sheep grazing and in reality should be dominated by dense gorse, heather and woodland.

"This project presents an exciting opportunity for a number of reasons. Firstly, there has been no large-scale rewilding of upland habitats in England to date, making this a pioneering project from an ecological perspective. Secondly, the Lowther Estate includes three large areas of upland suitable for rewilding (up to 5000 hectares each), meaning the spatial scope of this project is huge. Thirdly, there is a unique community element which to our knowledge would be the first of its kind anywhere in the UK. These areas of upland are common grazing land, an ancient land use system whereby local communities living on estate-owned land have the right to graze their livestock. The financial returns from grazing have severely diminished in recent years, significantly reducing income for the 'commoners', and so a main focus of this project would be to demonstrate how the rewilding of uplands can be used to financially compensate 'commoners' in return for restricting their grazing. In other words, it would allow us to show how the ancient practice of common grazing rights can be married to the modern concept of nature restoration."

But now let us head back to the trees and to Ben Abdelnoor who has a wonderful way with words, has kept a diary about life under Loughrigg, and who has given permission to use the following two extracts, both about trees.

> I ordered a copy of *Collins Complete Guide to British Trees* from my local bookshop. The book sat in various places around the house: the kitchen table, the lounge, bedside table. I occasionally flicked through it, waiting for the right time and a certain level of enthusiasm. For many years it frustrated me that I couldn't name, to a reasonable degree of certainty, more than four or five species. I wanted to know more. I started with some basic investigation of the trees that edged

the property and along the road at the end of the driveway. I didn't have to go far to find plenty: hazel, hawthorn, sycamore and yew. With some identification under my belt I felt a swell of satisfaction and searched for new ground.

I moved up to the woods at the back of the house, beyond the garden: oak, more hazel, Norway spruce and the answer as to why the neighbouring property is called *The Larches*. A brief wander beyond the woods and onto the fellside turned up rowan and hawthorn, with some recently planted oak and hazel saplings. By now I was eager to see what I could find beyond the boundaries of home. With a touch of excitement I headed up the road that ran alongside the river. Taking my time I was reasonably sure I'd identified elm and poplar, beech and maple. There were other species which looked interesting but I couldn't identify, so I'd take a leaf home, place it on the kitchen table, stare at it, then turn it over, all the while flicking through the pages of my handbook.

It was around this time that a friend mentioned his interest in trees. He proved to be as enthusiastic in helping me identify trees as I was enthusiastic about learning from him. I would send him images of parts of whichever tree I was struggling to identify: leaves, needles, trunk, cones, branches. In turn he'd often send me down a new line of inquiry: "Looks like a willow; grey willow leaves are longer than they are round." It didn't look to me like a willow but invariably he was right and I'm soon learning the minutiae of osier, goat, bay and grey willow.

On another walk a friend, working in the grounds of the doctor's surgery, pointed out a London plane. The circumference of its trunk is impressive, clearly displaying evidence of having been pollarded. The tree is huge, how had I never noticed it before? I've become distracted and perhaps a little obsessed. I can't walk anywhere without grinding to a halt to run my fingers over a leaf, looking for tufts of fine hair on the underside or visible glands on the petiole, to touch the bark or study the needles or cones. As I walk along I'll mutter under my breath a running commentary: beech, sycamore, oak, another beech, hazel…

And then he recalls the impact of Storm Arwen in November 2021, which wreaked a trail of devastation across Cumbria. Swathes of forest and woodland were destroyed, taken out by strong northerly winds gusting at over 70 mph.

I used to live beneath Loughrigg, on the back road to Rydal, just across the narrow footbridge from Rothay Park. It was a wonderful location; from our back garden you could wander up through the woods – Douglas fir, Sitka spruce, larch and rhododendron – clamber over the gate at the top, and be on the lower slopes of Todd Crag.

In the years that I lived at *The Hollies* I spent hundreds of hours up in those woods, especially the glade towards the top. Here it flattened out and the tallest trees encircled a patch of grass and soft moss that invited a blanket to be laid down as it caught the afternoon sun. I would lie in this open space on Sunday afternoons, alternating between dozing off and reading a book. Some nights we'd buy fish and chips in the village and wander up through the trees to sit and enjoy them in the fading light.

I learned to identify many of the trees along the wooded slopes, investigated old quarry workings, quietly stalked deer, picked wild garlic and wood sorrel in spring or played hide-and-seek with the dog. Living there and having those woods brought me so much happiness.

Now those woods have all but gone. They've been swept over, as if felled by one almighty hand. Toppled, one against the other, a set of dominoes collapsed and never to be set right again. It's heart-breaking to see and I couldn't bring myself to visit until now, five months after Arwen has done its damage. I cautiously pick my way down through the woods, hoping to have a quick look before the race (Loughrigg fell race). I step over the gate at the property's boundary with the fell, itself crushed beneath an ancient oak. I haul myself over huge trunks, scraping my thighs and scratching my arms in the process. I clamber beneath trees, pushing past tangles of roots and upended bushes. It's hard to work out what I can safely stand on as it's still so fresh and precarious. I haven't appreciated quite how difficult this terrain is to move through when you can barely stand on the ground itself, hopping from trunk to branch and trying not to slip through the gaps. I arrive at the area where the open patch of woodland was, now just a pile of jauntily angled fir and pine trees. It's ugly and depressing.

There's more about Ben and a den in the woods to come. But on a more positive note, early in 2024 the young trees planted on Todd Crag have had willow warblers singing from them, and there was a whitethroat in a scrubby patch too. Over the last few years there have been skylarks heard singing on Loughrigg after a gap of many years. The numbers of bird's eye primroses found flowering has been well over 1000 in recent three years. And for the specialists, the rainforest indicator lichen *Cetrelia olivetorum* has been found spreading onto a new tree above Brow Head.

Soundtrack: Blackbird, The Beatles

CHAPTER FOUR

THE FOLKS WHO LIVE ON THE HILL

Ophelia Almond and her twin brother Alfie have been playing on Loughrigg since they could walk. "I have a mountain for a back garden, and a swimming pool opposite the house," says Ophelia, as we sit looking out over Loughrigg Tarn. "It's perfect."

They live in an estate cottage rented from the National Trust with father Dave, who is gardens and outdoors manager for the Trust based at Fell Foot country park at the foot of Windermere, and mother Becky Heaton Cooper, director of the Heaton Cooper Studio in Grasmere. She's an artist "with very little time to paint", descended from the grand masters of Lake District painting, great grandfather Alfred Heaton Cooper, grandfather William Heaton Cooper, and her grandmother, Ophelia Gordon Bell, a sculptor.

Dave was already living in the house, Becky moved in shortly before the twins were born, and so it was perfectly normal that one of their first outings as babies was in a double papoose strapped onto Dave to the summit of Loughrigg, just a 20-minute climb from their back gate.

We were sitting in the front garden on a warm autumn

afternoon, Dave digging weeds as we talked, Ophelia – an elegant and composed young woman, still in shorts on this day – lounging beside us. Alfie was excused: "He's sitting inside with a pack of frozen peas on his nose," explained Becky. "There was an incident at a rugby match this morning."

Brought up in Ambleside, Becky moved to Grasmere after studying art in Newcastle. She's a smart, fashionable businesswoman, equally at home in the galleries of London and her own Cumbrian studio, but this house at the foot of a mountain is her corner of heaven. "I grew up at the other side of the hill and it was always our playground. It's a remarkable hill. If I could never go up anywhere else apart from Loughrigg, it would be OK.

"I've been exploring that hill since I was a kid, on my bike, climbing little crags, getting into all sorts of trouble. Playing around for hours and hours. It's always been my favourite fell. And when we go exploring as a family now, since when the kids were younger, you can always find somewhere you've not been before.

"There have been times when I've ended up in a bit of a pickle, but it wasn't really dangerous. I remember once me and Alfie following a wall up, he was probably only about 7, and we did start to get into a scramble, almost vertical, on rock, and I remember thinking, please do not tell your dad about this, Alfie. But we got to the top and we got down safely again."

Dave has lived in the Lakes since age of 14 and before moving here he was in Grasmere, at the end of Easedale Road on the way to Helm Crag, "though the cottage was dark and there was narrow sky". Like a hobbit house, says Ophelia. "We have big sky here."

He's not one for following paths, unless it's necessary. "We have two very distinct seasons here. When the bracken is up we go on the path like everyone else. Then come the end of this month (September) we get our boots on and we never go on a path. We follow sheep trods, we might cross a path now and again. We just find our own way." The family has camped out on Loughrigg, and Ophelia has ideas about stringing a hammock between two trees for the next time. One summer Dave and the children slept in the garden for a few weeks. Now Alfie has started going off on his own for evening adventures, with a camping stove and a stash of drinking chocolate, and snacks. Says Becky: "I just love the fact he's got his confidence to go, it's like a rite of passage."

Is it not a remote place for a teenager to live, I ask Ophelia? "I like it because it's not over-run with people. But there is a sense of community, when you go for a walk and chat with people, or they talk when passing by here. On the other hand, it's not really near friends' houses but they don't live too far away so it's not a big problem." I ask her how she would feel about living elsewhere, implying that she might one day go to college in Manchester or London: "I wouldn't MIND living in Ambleside, or Grasmere." She likes Lily Tarn "because you can run up there and not have to speak to anybody".

And yet this was proving to be a sociable afternoon, many passers-by on the bridle path stopping for a chat. One eventually stops for half an hour and proves to be a local expert on Loughrigg. He's Paul Burke, a member of the Langdale Ambleside Mountain Rescue Team, of which Dave Almond was once a member. Becky says: "It's a very warm community. We're dispersed around the tarn, not on top of each other, but yet there's a lovely sense of community."

Dave says: "Living and working locally, there are a lot of plus points being part of a local community, but here we have that without the local politics. They are all estate houses, people are in the same situation with the same landlord, it's uncomplicated, everybody's in the same kind of accommodation, there's no big homeowners, nobody wealthier than *yow*. It's a homogenous community. And there's a whole community of people who don't live here but come back year after year and have a sense of ownership of the hill, a strong community of long-distance locals. We get to know people who come past while on holiday."

During lockdown the children, with parental guidance, produced several copies of *The Loughrigg Times*, a print magazine which included much from their school syllabus: science, history, biology, English. "It was a vehicle for the curriculum when they were being taught at home" says Dave. Highlights included features about lizards and adders that they saw, and the owl babies in a local tree.

Becky adds: "You don't have to go far to see something wonderful. We go up from our back gate to the primrose walk, a great big raft of primroses in the spring. You might see a fox walking past. Every time you go out, there's a different aspect, every time we walk up there it's from a different angle. It's a family favourite, it's *our* family favourite."

And always has been. Her grandfather, William Heaton Cooper, loved Loughrigg. In *The Hills of Lakeland* he wrote:

> It is typical of the low hills that children adopt as their favourite playground. On it are innumerable hills and valleys and shallow tarns which appear and disappear and freeze earlier than the big sheets of water.... For many years my father had a small hut just below the summit where we would go and camp for days on end, living like savages, cooking on a trench oven, swimming in the tarns and falling off rocks – the very best holiday education for youngsters. We would sleep out on the dry turf in the heat of summer and wake up with dew on our faces.

What's it like, living on Loughrigg, on the hill itself, I ask Gary Gibson? "Heaven. Absolute heaven," he replies. Gary and his wife Sharon live at Pine Rigg, the newly-built eco-friendly, gorgeously-weathered house by the second gate on the way up Loughrigg on the bridleway from Ambleside. At the 500ft contour they are, literally, halfway to the summit, in a home that faces east, a home that's the essence of peace and harmony. "It feels like we are living 50 miles away from the next human being, yet it's less than a mile as the crow flies from the middle of Ambleside. We have everything we need on the doorstep, but it doesn't seem like that. It's the golden key."

Pine Rigg is a house with history, and it's delightful to see the friendship that's developed between the couple living their dream here and the last remaining resident of the previous owners, in what was originally a golf club house. "I'm a very lucky man. They look after me so well," says Pete Deeley who lived here on the site for 50 years. So we start with his story, a biography full of adventure, friendship and romance. Pete's now 90, and though his eyesight is failing, his memories are sharp and clear. Originally from Lancaster, Pete teamed up with three other climbers who met at a party. Two couples who, early on, swapped partners. Pete was married to Monica, but fell in love with Joan, who was married to Bryan, who fell in love with Monica. And so developed an unorthodox, sensible, pragmatic arrangement in which the four of them pooled resources in a sort of communal living.

They were, naturally, considered local 'characters'. "At the time it was a bit of a sensation, but the arrangement was permanent and we stayed together, Joan and I, for 53 years which is longer than a lot of marriages last these days." Divorce, then, was "fiendishly expensive and very adversarial" so the girls changed their names by deed poll.

Together they set up the Lakeland Mountaineering School, and together – after living in converted barns and cow byres and boat houses – they found the funds and a mortgage to buy the golf club house. "We wanted a base for our climbing school as well as a home. It was the perfect solution, it was the most magical place." A magical place with only calor gas and no electricity, back in 1963. "I remember standing with Bryan on the bottom lawn, looking at the house and saying, if we can get this I'd spend the rest of my life here."

A founder member of the Ambleside Mountain Rescue team, which later merged with Langdale, Pete's had many careers – builder, plumber, taxi-driver, steeplejack, swing-band musician – but in his adult life, just this one home till he moved into a retirement apartment in the centre of Ambleside a few years ago. The group of four friends bought the place for £5000, a reduced price following the seriously severe winter of 1962/3. The building had been the club house for a nine-hole golf course "though more of a fell walk than a round of golf".

Pete has shared his memories with the Ambleside Oral History archive, and here recalls issues to do with the water supply, and power.

What happened when the water ran dry during droughts in summer? Funnily enough, we were there for 50 years, and it only ran out maybe three, at most four times. I don't think it even ran out in 1976 (the year of notorious drought). I don't think people appreciate water. They take it for granted, and until you've lived without electricity and certainly without water when it runs out, that is by far the worst. You don't realise how much water it takes to flush a toilet and even to carry it in a bucket, it's heavy. So you learn all sorts of dodges… . We had a little indicator, or what they say in these parts, a gab eye. On the road there was a bit of a rock end that used to run with water all the time. If it got to summer and it was dry, the patch of water slowly diminished in size and eventually during the day it would vanish totally, totally dry. Next morning, overnight, there'd be a little patch of water. Once that happened then it's up to the tank, lift the lid and have a look in, and there'd be a slow drip and once that happened, you'd know you'd got maybe a week to ten days if the weather doesn't break. But when it dries up altogether, then it's desperate.

The power supply was another 'adventure'.

We had calor gas, which we cooked on, and for lighting, and eventually we bought a diesel generator.… . and finally in 1970 the North Western Electricity Board as it then was, wrote and said 'how about having electricity'. It was like winning the pools. So we said 'yes please!' I think it cost us £250.… . Good thing is, it arrived in 1970, fantastic, put a switch down – light comes on, I've never forgotten the feeling, absolutely wonderful. But electricity on poles isn't really a good idea living in a mountainous area because of wind, snow, ice etc, so fairly regularly it used to go off. But by this time you make allowances don't you. You have candles, torches, calor gas, stuff that we'd kept, so it wasn't a massive problem, just a flaming nuisance.

The golf club house was basically a wooden shack with a stone built extension at the back with kitchen, bathroom, and two bedrooms. It had been built in 1903 on the formation of the Ambleside and District Golf Club. The links were laid out on land leased from Brow Head Farm with the agreement of the tenant, Anthony Chapman. The nine-hole course was designed by the Lytham and St Annes professional, Mr Lowe "and a suitable pavilion erected". *https://www.golfsmissinglinks.co.uk/*

"A wooden shack with all the problems that a timber constructed house has unless you keep on top of it." After 50 years, and with only Pete and Monica still alive, the house was in a poor state of repair. "The southern gable end was rotten, it was full of woodworm, it needed a lot of attention, a lot."

And so the house and its 1.75 acres of land went on the market and in time – three years, in fact – the plot was bought by Sharon and Gary who were living in the Midlands. Sharon had worked in HR, Gary worked for a software company, and they have five children, two of Gary's and three of Sharon's from a previous marriage, one of whom was still at school at that time. They were looking to re-locate and only considered the Lakes after staying in Ambleside and visiting friends in Grasmere, who teach meditation. This is an important part of their lives, and had an impact on the design of the new house that they were to build on the Pine Rigg site. They wanted an east facing house.

"We travelled up on a really grey day. We had no idea what was there," Sharon recalls. "There could have been a Sainsburys over the hill for all we knew. And the bridleway was in such a poor state that the estate agent refused to drive up it." The silence, she said, hit her, but in spite of the absence of any view, she knew instantly it was where she wanted to live." Now, of course, they know intimately what lies beyond their gate and regularly climb to the summit of their own hill.

The sale was completed in August 2014, and Sharon's son Scott, who had been to university in Preston, moved in with his girlfriend, Jade, while plans were made, an architect hired, and Gary became the manager of the project. Demolition of the old building started in August 2016, and it was two years later that the couple moved into their new home.

They hired architect Ben Cunliffe, whose ideas were tempered by Sharon and Gary's needs, particularly for a meditation room which had to be in the north-east corner of the house. "We had very specific ideas about what we wanted," said Gary, who explained about Sthapatya-Veda design. This is an ancient system of knowledge that involves the connection between people and the buildings in which they live and work. It is similar to the Chinese concept of feng shui. In Sthapatya-Veda, the belief is that the design of the structure has an effect on one's prana, life force energy. If the design of the building is in harmony with the laws of nature, it will promote positive energy. "And that's what we've created, a home that's harmonious, secure, peaceful."

They incorporated whatever they could from the former golf club building, and used two felled cedar trees as timber for part of the interior. The building work took two years, then during the pandemic lockdown they added a tree house in the garden for their grandchildren. "We tried to re-use as much of the old house as possible," says Sharon.

Pete Deeley says: "It's now a beautiful home. Those two massive cedar trees, they had to be felled, much to my delight, they were far too close to the house. I think three times I had to get ladders out to try and cut the boughs which were overhanging the house, which was crazy. Now there are places in the house where he's used the planks that came from those cedars."

Pete has great affection for what they've done, and for Sharon and Gary themselves, an affection that's clearly mutual. They made him a bowl from one of the cedar planks: "So I'm now in my comfortable flat in Ambleside, looking at a little piece of Pine Rigg that I looked at for fifty years and that's lovely. And that's the sort of people they are. It's now a home that they built and love, and put their own character into it."

He had so much knowledge to pass on from his 50 years living on the hill. "One of the first things I did was to explain about the water, so they had a bore hole drilled, to solve the problems." And he advised them to keep on top of repairs to the access road, which the postman and other delivery drivers are clearly happy about now.

Gary says: "We can really connect with wildlife here. There's nothing else to distract you, no one to take your attention away. We have time to see it all and appreciate it." They still have an occasional visit from a stoat, a family of which had been living between the walls in the old house. Other regular visitors include mice, voles, badgers, red and roe deer, and red squirrels.

Trees have fallen down in recent years, particularly during Storm Arwen in 2021, but the house now looks embedded into the landscape. Pete says: "The house sits beautifully in the site and the atmosphere is still there and the wood hasn't changed, the big intake field hasn't changed, where the golf tees are. And the view of the Fairfield Horseshoe hasn't changed."

Ben Abdelnoor would go to sleep looking out onto Loughrigg with the door open. Strictly speaking, there was no door, just an open side of the rough shelter in the woods behind his house at the foot of the hill. Later, his housemate John Hempston, an "amazing handyman", built a much bigger cabin from fallen trees, dragging their trunks through the woods, and Ben put in a camping mattress. Like all the best people in life, he's never really grown up.

For several years Ben, baker by profession, exceptional fellrunner by gift, lived on the lower slopes of the hill that he calls an "overground rabbit warren". He's won many of the big races in the Lake District, over mountains like Scafell Pike and Pillar and Great Gable, and now lives in the shadow of majestic Blencathra, near Threlkeld, but his heart belongs to Loughrigg. "If I had to choose, I'd say it was my favourite fell."

He'd been living in the centre of Ambleside and wanted to move out of town; the house near Miller Bridge came up to let when friends of Ben's from the running club were moving away. "It was ideal for me and two friends. There was a huge window, with one massive pane of glass, looking across to Wansfell. There were deer on the lawn; they created a network of tunnels through the rhododendrons in the garden. A sparrowhawk would come to the bird feeder. And when I was coming back from a run in the dark, I'd do signals with my head torch. Back in the house, my friends could see my light on the summit of Wansfell."

Ben set up a slack line between trees in the garden. For a while he kept hens in the garden inspired by a big black cockerel that turned up at the back door; but then a stoat or a weasel finished them off. He'd see otters in the river. And from the back door he'd head off up the steep climb through the woods onto Loughrigg, always a different route.

During lockdown, Ben says, the hill and the woods helped preserve his sanity. "I kept thinking about people living in high rise flats, in cities. We were so fortunate." In the log-cabin in the garden he'd sit and read, and for a while "I tried to work out how to build a dry stone wall." The cabin, built by house-mate John, with whom Ben lived for ten years, was based on an Adirondack shelter, a three-sided log structure popularised in the Adirondack Mountains of Upstate New York which provides shelter for campers.

John says: "It came about because I enjoy building and spending purposeful time outdoors and then it gave me somewhere convenient to sleep in the fresh air occasionally. I had intended to take a course in Sweden to learn the traditional process of jointing logs in the summer of 2020 but when news of a potential lockdown came along I saw the opportunity to teach myself. The specialist tools got ordered and delivered just before shops closed and I researched building techniques online. Late March to early May 2020 were a really blissful time for me in many ways. I spent much of the time alone up in our woods above the house.

It was quite hard work but I could go at a very natural pace without any strict deadlines."

From a diary entry at the time, Ben shares this:

> From my lofty slope in the garden I can look out across a sleeping town. The soft glow of house lights and street lights brings to mind the image of a South American favela, except there is no sound of gunfire, car exhausts, loud music or shouting. Save for the occasional barking of a dog the town lies under a muffled silence until first light, whereupon a dawn chorus begins soon after 4am.

It was also in a lockdown-diary that Ben recalled his good friend Chris Stirling, who died in April 2019. "Chris was an internationally-successful triathlete, winner of the Celtman race, although *his* mountain was nearby Wansfell, which he aimed to run up each day before 7am. In the afternoon I meet with two friends to remember Chris. We sit in the drizzle, in a small clearing reached by a short climb through woods from the back of the house. We sit, talk and drink a beer to Chris which, looking back, were three things Chris didn't do very much of."

Ben says he always felt like a character from a Richmal Crompton book, being *Just William* playing in the woods. One evening he decided to burn some rhododenrons that he'd been clearing from the woods at the back of the garden. He'd got a good fire going, safely away from other trees, when he saw what he describes as "three guys dressed as Ghostbusters. It took me a minute to realise it was the local volunteer fire service. They'd had reports about smoke. But they saw what I was doing, safely, and marked it down as 'false alarm with good intent'."

The log cabin escaped being hit by trees, many of which fell during the night of Storm Arwen in November 2021. "It was a miracle really, because so many trees came down in that part of the wood. The whole landscape up there has changed now, paths disappeared. It was very powerful."

National Trust rangers and forestry teams at the time said they faced an "emotional" job clearing fallen trees in the Lake District. Thousands were brought down when Arwen hit the area with severe winds causing chaos, particularly around Ambleside. The main track up to Loughrigg from Miller Bridge was blocked at Loughrigg Brow, a house under Loughrigg north of the cattlegrid had an iconic monkey-puzzle tree fall on its roof, and many homes in the area were without power for up to a week. It was the unusual direction of the wind, barreling through the Rydal valley from the Fairfield Horsehoe, the north, experts said, that caused so much damage, not the usual direction against which the trees had rooted over many many years.

Ancient oak, beech, pine, spruce, sequoia and wild cherry were uprooted. Trees were left leaning at angles; trees had their trunks split, branches ripped away. Larch plantations were reduced to what looked like matchsticks. Homes, fences, and stone walls were battered and broken and tiles ripped from rooftops. I remember that night well. We often talk, glibly, about sleeplessness, about not having a wink of sleep, but that night it was genuinely impossible to sleep because of the noise, and the fear that with every gust a tree would crash down on my roof, particularly the roof of the conservatory.

In the morning my own damage was minimal; all the ceramic plant pots had been blown off the window ledge and lay smashed in the front garden. Across the street, the roof of a neighbour's garden shed had been lifted, carried over the top of her house, and deposited in the roadway, inches from my parked car. But of more immediate concern was the Owl. At first light several of us ran across to the foot of Loughrigg, climbed recklessly over fallen trees and scrambled up the Brow to check if the tree that houses the owl's nest had survived. It had, though many around it were brought down that night.

We've got used to the changed landscape. We walk and run past giant uprooted trees lying on their sides, with a sense of wonder still, but they have become familiar. It's a new habitat for wildlife, it's an altered view, it's a prompt to memory of how things used to be. But for Chris and Siobhan Routledge it was the night of Storm Desmond back in December 2015 that was a far more traumatic experience. They woke to find the river Rothay had burst its banks, crossed the Under Loughrigg road to their garden steps, and washed their car a hundred metres downstream, leaving it propped up, nose down, against a tree.

There was a very distinct silver lining to these clouds for Chris, a photographer. He spent days capturing images of the flooded fields, the stranded sheep, the altered landscape, and his pictures ultimately became part of a three year project in which he documented the landscape around the Rothay river valley. The photographs explore some of the strange and beautiful effects of the flood, from crushed fences and knitted debris, to sodden ground, and turf rolled up by the force of the water.

Storm Desmond was the most powerful of recent Atlantic storms, blowing in across Great Britain and Ireland, bringing with it violent winds and extreme rainfall. Flooding and high winds closed railway lines and roads, and many areas were without power, some for several days. In Cumbria, one of the worst-hit English counties, 34 centimetres of rain fell in one day, by some margin a record for a 24-hour period in Britain. Following the storm, news media naturally focused on damage to bridges, roads, railway lines and buildings, piles of ruined furniture, and the inadequacy of flood defences; the imagery was dramatic, and the stories often heartbreaking.

"For some of us, the aftermath was a quieter affair," Chris recalls. "As the floodwater went down I set about photographing what the storm left behind on a short stretch of the river Rothay at Rydal: flattened vegetation, debris hanging high up in trees, the transformation of the landscape. It seemed to me, wandering the nearby woods and riverbank, that this land was an indeterminate land; both of the river, and not of it. Ordinarily it is a pretty, quiet, benign landscape, where people stop to take selfies, but it is also one that transforms within hours into a raging flood. And that the flooding itself is also a cleansing, a sweeping through of what humans, and nature, have left behind." A book of the photos was produced, and the project was exhibited at the Heaton Cooper Studio Archive Gallery in October 2019.

Chris and Siobhan have grown to understand the river and to recognise when, and how deeply, it might flood after heavy rainfall, when to move their car to high ground, and to realise that walking home with overtopped boots is a commonplace. "There is a kind of pattern, you can see what it's going to do fairly accurately."

But the water they rely on, their water supply, comes from behind the house, from Loughrigg itself. Their home is built, literally, into the fabric of the mountain, the back wall of their boots-and-coats room is a rock face. It's part of the house; all the houses around here are made from stone around them. "All the houses along here back onto the hill, it's the view of Wansfell and the river that they were built for, but we are nestled in it, we are part of it." As are Marx and Engels, the gerbils who died within a few weeks of each other and are buried at the back on the hill, in a little bit of woodland.

"We know when it's dry up on the fell, because our water doesn't flow. And we know when it's frozen up there, too." During the drought in the summer of 2023, says Chris, the birds normally found on the fellside were down beside the river in front of their house. "Stonechats, meadow pippits, all the ones that are usually on the top of the fell, were down here competing with the robins and the blackbirds."

The stone to build the house, dated 1855, a small part of a bigger mansion, came from the quarries on Loughrigg. "But there was a farmhouse here on the site many hundreds of years ago. It's had lots of lives. It's been a yeoman's cottage."

Loughrigg is their playground. Siobhan picks up an ordinary tea tray: "This is the summit tray. At weekends, on high days and holidays, we take drinks and nibbles upstairs to the sitting room. But on a fine summer's evening we'll pack all that into a rucksack and have a gin and tonic, a little bowl of olives, some crisps, and take them up to the summit of the fell. It's our outdoor sitting room." Chris says: "During a working day when we break off to go for a walk, that's where we go, it's the obvious place to go. This whole side of it, the shoulder, takes about an hour from here. Which is why it's so lovely for a summer evening walk before dinner. And on Christmas Day."

When their daughter Caitlin was tiny, maybe two years old, she insisted on walking up to the top, and all the way down. Soon after that she found, on a subsidiary summit, her armchair, a little step in the rock, and she wanted to visit it and sit there. "She had an imaginary house there. But latterly we have used it almost as an extension to the house, as an extra room.

"The hill protects us. When there's heavy snowfall, it can be knee deep up on the hill behind us and only a few centimetres here in the garden. The snow is being held back from falling on us." And yet, says Siobhan, "though we live on Loughrigg, we can't see it. It's Wansfell we look out onto at the front." Chris adds: "It's like living right underneath the Eiffel Tower."

Caitlin, now a student at York University, has started wandering solo on Loughrigg, and in the summer of 2023 she camped out one night on the hill. She didn't see a soul, although there were some people swimming in Rydal the next morning.

Chris says: "From a photographer's viewpoint, it's fascinating. There's lots of little gullies, dips, bits of forest and woodland, little bits of wet land, lots of birds, there are some lovely shapes, and of course the pine trees, and it's starting to change. There are quarries, a landscape that's been worked, and far fewer sheep now so there are new trees coming through. It's the start of a natural regeneration, a healthy situation. One of the best photos I've ever taken is of a wild cherry on Loughrigg, which is really beautiful."

The weather often dominates conversation, but Chris says: "I especially like living with the river and its moods. The weather is bigger; you can see it moving, like a herd of large animals, across the landscape."

Paul Mann also lives under Loughrigg. A runner with Kendal Athletic Club, he's proprietor of the Fox Ghyll country house B&B, a guest house with a fascinating history whose residents have included Thomas de Quincey and William Edward Forster, a 19th century Minister for Education. And Paul is Lord of the Manor of Loughrigg. It's not something he brags about among friends, and it's certainly not a title he uses on his passport or any other official documents. But it's a title he inherited from his father, Timothy Mann, who himself bought it when auctioned by the Lowther Estate in

1988. Since 2008 the Lordship is titular only, although at the time that Timothy Mann secured it, there were rights and privileges, including the right to fish and hunt.

Paul grew up in Ambleside, after his parents bought Fox Ghyll when he was just one year old. It's a rather splendid Regency building surrounded by trees, just off the road, opposite another historic house, Fox Howe. It's a Grade 2 listed building, which has much older original parts. Alterations and additions are thought to have been the work of Robert Blakeney (1758-1822), who was a friend of William Wordsworth. And another friend of Wordsworth, the essayist and journalist and, briefly, editor of the *Westmorland Gazette*, Thomas de Quincey, lived there from 1820-1825. De Quincey was an essayist and journalist best remembered for his *Confessions of an English Opium Eate*r. Fox Ghyll was later the home of William Forster, Liberal MP for Bradford, after whom the city's Forster Square is named, and whose 1870 Education Act laid the foundations for primary schools. He married the daughter of Thomas Arnold, Headmaster of Rugby school, who built nearby Fox How (and who left that estate to his son Matthew, the poet, writer and educationalist).

Paul's parents started to run Fox Ghyll as a guest house in 1980, initially offering dinner as well as bed and breakfast, as was customary then; Ambleside had few restaurants other than in hotels which served residents only, and pub food back then, reminds Paul, meant crisps and pickled eggs. He went to school in Ambleside, and then to The Lakes secondary school at Troutbeck Bridge. And throughout his childhood

Loughrigg was where he played out. "We would go off for hours on end, playing in the woods, building dens and tree houses. I guess that's why I take it for granted; it was always there." Their neighbour had been a veterinary scientist who had developed vaccines for chickens in a shed, which Paul can remember visiting as a child when it was derelict. Also within their grounds was a very basic outward bound hut, built by the head teacher of Silcoates School and used by generations of schoolchildren and Duke of Edinburgh award youngsters, and latterly by Paul's friends and family. But that was crushed by a fallen tree during Storm Arwen.

"There were always plenty of fallen trees behind the house. We had a donkey called Jack which used to drag fallen logs down the hillside to feed a wood-burning boiler." After leaving school Paul had a small business venture running a sweet shop next to the Low Fold car park in Ambleside, before heading to Leeds University to study broadcast and media, and subsequently making a career as a freelance cameraman, working throughout the UK. But he always gravitated back to Fox Ghyll, and came home to help his mother after his father's death, where those landscaped gardens give direct access to Loughrigg Fell. When the guest house had to close during the pandemic lockdown, Paul started a sideline selling ice-cream at the gate. "It was good fun during the summer, I got to meet people passing by, because there's not many people live permanently along here."

He's coy about his 'lordship' although he's proud that it is a real title "and not one of those things you can buy off the internet, like a slice of the moon. It's a proper manorial title which originally had fishing rights and hunting rights and mineral rights. My father bought it in the 1980s when the Lowther Estate put on a big auction, so I inherited it, though I never did anything with it. And now the authorities have stripped away any powers that go with it. But I do remember my father being called by the utilities, the electricity or water boards, if they were putting up pylons or installing new pipework, and they had to consult him." It applied to the whole of Loughrigg, including the Tarn. "It's an important historic document, even though we actually own only about ten acres of land now. It was the jewel in the crown of the Lowther estate when my father bought it."

Soundtrack: The folks who live on the hill, Peggy Lee

CHAPTER FIVE

THE RUNNERS' PLAYGROUND

There is a joy in running fast downhill over rough ground that transcends any other kind of euphoria. In recent years, apart from on Loughrigg, I've experienced that sensation for just about 100m during the Whinlatter Forest parkrun, when the route deviates suddenly from the main track and drops steeply down through woods on a narrow, tree-rooted path before a U-turn and another climb.

In the fellrunning world I was never a great descender, too fearful to relax fully and put the brain into neutral. Watching great downhill runners is a joy in itself, the elegance of their balance, the grace of their instinctive step-finding. Only once did I do the Ben Nevis race and somewhere on a near-vertical slope above the Red Burn, the front-runners came hurtling towards me and in a split second I realised that THEY couldn't get out of MY way. These days, in trail races, and parkruns, I do make a little downhill progress; it's all relative.

Loughrigg has it all, for the novice and the mountain goat alike, rocky paths, stretches of bog, straight sections, winding tracks, all contained in a short space. The eponymous

race route, from the centre of Rothay Park and back, is
just four miles, the steepest and most painful section being
the tarmac path on Loughrigg Brow just above the cattle
grid at Miller Bridge. Ever more slowly I would 'run' to the
summit, sometimes overtaken by a strong walker, often in the
knowledge that if I changed to a walk, I could ascend more
quickly. But stubborn pride persists.

I would usually take the same route, the shortest way
to the top from Ambleside, past Pine Rigg, then after the fell
gate turn right (first bog, briefly bridged by a precarious strip
of wood) then left, up and across another bog and then the
beck at Troughton Gill, the short-cut just after a cairn on the
left which I dubbed 'the sometimes pond', a small descent,
then up through 'No Man's Land' to the steps which lead to
the summit. No, I never counted them. Usually I would run
alone, as no one else locally ran as slowly as I did. Even the
late great Roger Bell, by then into his 80s, disappeared from
view during an informal time trial organised by Ambleside
AC runners during one of the pandemic lockdowns, all of us
setting off at the same time. Roger, recalls John Gomersall,
"couldn't find his stopwatch so he brought an alarm clock."

But I did join a joyous downhill party back in the
summer of 2019 when another Ambleside AC legend, Paul
Tierney, was on track to set a new record for running all the
Wainwrights. I was helping behind the scenes, in the 'crow's
nest' they called it, organising food and kit, passing messages
from those on the run supporting Paul to those waiting to
take their turn, monitoring his progress summit by summit.

On the Sunday afternoon, a bright but cold day, I wanted to see some of the action and went up onto Loughrigg to wait for Paul and his companions to pass through. A quick tap of the trig point with a walking pole, and he was off at a gallop down past Rydal cave to a rest point at the Badger Bar, followed by a dozen supporters and me tagging along at the back.

Jim Tyson recalls what happened after that, when Paul set off over the Fairfield range heading for Kirkstone Pass. "This was June, but the weather was brutal. There were 16 of us set off on the next leg, and it was so grim, there was such a storm blowing, and people dropped out one by one, they were getting hypothermic. There was horizontal rain, and with head torches on it was just white streaks glowing across your face." Eventually just Jim and Dan Duxbury remained when Paul finally reached the end of that section after daybreak.*

Jim, an Ambleside AC stalwart and childhood winner of the local Rushbearing fell race, had included Loughrigg many times during a very special personal challenge in 2015, when he ran at least 5k every day for 365 days in memory of his father who had died the previous year. He was raising money for Parkinsons UK. "It was a very good year, very cathartic." He also built into the year's running the ascent of the three highest British peaks, Snowdon and Ben Nevis and Scafell Pike, and added Snaefell on the Isle of Man for good measure.

Caricatures of his running friends and colleagues appear occasionally in Jim's eagerly-anticipated Fell Runners' Calendar, which combines his cartooning talent with his love of the hills. Loughrigg may well be there in the background.

"It's an elevated playground, a place for adventures. It's a wonderful fell."

The locals for whom Loughrigg is, literally, their playground are the junior runners of Ambleside Athletic Club. Parents, dog-walkers, passers-by will have seen them gather in Rothay Park on a Thursday evening to set off on a training run, some as young as eight years old. The parents are the ones who see them return an hour later, happy and covered in mud. What happens in that time sounds like the most wonderful fun a child could have.

Niki Rylance was junior co-ordinator of the fell running squad for 10 years, initially working with another senior runner and then solo. She holds qualifications in Leadership in Fell Running, Coaching Assistant, first aid, and other fell-specific training. A physiotherapist by profession, she's married to a running GP, and they have two famously long-legged and very glamorous running daughters. Chloe, now studying sport at university in the USA, started running when she was 8. She has been English junior fell-running champion several times, and has run for England on "umpteen" occasions. Sophie is also heading to study sport in the USA, and she's also run for England, and – after turning 18 – took part in senior events such as the Langdale and Three Shires races, as well as being a member of the successful Ambleside women's team. The sisters have represented England at the international Sky championships in Italy, running against youngsters from all over the world. And this, says Niki, is thanks to an early life spent on Loughrigg. "Running is what we do as a family. It's our life. When we go on holiday we go to the mountains, and when we're at home we run on Loughrigg."

The mountain has everything a novice runner could need. It's accessible, the terrain is varied and, as Niki explains, the children play games without even realising they are 'training'.

"It's just there. For the little ones, especially those whose parents might not be outdoorsy themselves, they see it as a proper mountain. It might be a major expedition for a seven-year-old to get to Lily Tarn. The older ones can get all the way to the top of Loughrigg. It's got something for everybody."

The children, says Niki, have their own names for different bits of the fell. "Todd Crag has little summits which the youngsters call the Knobbly Bobblies. We've organised relays to the top, we play *Capture the Flag* where, unknowingly, they are doing hill sprints. We have races up and down the little gullies, and many relays around Lily Tarn for all age groups. In the summer the little ones might go for a swim in Lily Tarn even though it's a bit sludgy. I remember Luke Bowen trying so hard in a relay, cutting the corner, that he fell in." Tom Ashworth, allegedly, fell in deliberately on more than one occasion. It was Tom, out for a run with his father, the mountain and race photographer Steve Ashworth, who wanted to go for a swim in the tarn. In winter. "We've no spare kit so the only way you can do that is if you take all your clothes off," Steve warned. Which Tom duly did.

Niki Rylance talks of playing games such as *Grandma's Footsteps* where the runners hide in the bracken, "and there's one wonderful muddy slope they called Skiddy Hill where they play a game called *sticks of doom*. They think it's great fun. It comes into its own when there's snow when they come down as penguins – on their tummies.

"And bogs! The kids love bogs. One was named after Maisie Evans after she face planted in it. They love getting filthy. They do triple jumps over the bogs and ask, can we do it again? It's games, but it's learning to be safe on the fells, teaching them navigation, experiencing every weather condition. We go up in the dark, with head torches. One of the coaches who's in the Mountain Rescue Team has a storm shelter and he takes it up onto the hill so they can experience that. It's not just running.

"You get special moments, standing at the top of Todd Crag in the dark, and the children turn their head torches off, and they see Ambleside below them like a tiny alpine village."

But it's also the hill where runners are selected for the British teams. The junior races staged on the fell, to Todd Crag or Lily Tarn, include English championship events and GB selection trials as well as junior club championship events, and the Rushbearing Race. Rushbearing is a festival celebration associated with the ancient custom of annually replacing the rushes on the earth floors of churches, rushes being a general term for reeds and sweet-smelling grasses. Once widespread throughout the Lake District, very few places now continue the tradition.

Ambleside Rushbearing is a community event. The bearings
vary from large ornate devices such as hoops, staves and
crosses to simple sheaves carried by children. Composed
mainly of rushes cut from nearby lake shores, they are highly
decorated with mosses, flowers and greenery. And afterwards,
youngsters who have taken part in the parade are eligible
to run in a race up and down Todd Crag. The boy and girl
winners both get trophies, the boys' one being named after
Clive Braithwaite who ran the course in 10 minutes 32
seconds in the 1970s, a record which still stands.

For senior runners, there are many races that go up, over
or around Loughrigg, the namesake event being the four-mile
race staged on a Wednesday night in April, shortly after the
clocks have gone forward and there's enough light for runners
to head there and back safely, straight to the top and back
down to Rothay Park. Within those four miles (6.4k) there's
1080 ft/330m of climbing. Jacob Adkin holds the men's record
of 25.26, set in 2021, and Sarah McCormack ran the fastest
women's time of 29.39 back in 2017.

It's categorised by the Fell Runners' Association as
AS. Specifically, 'A' races should average not less than 50
metres of climbing per kilometre, should not have more than
20% of the race distance on road, and should be at least 1.5k
in length. 'S' means Short races, less than 10k in length. And
that's where Loughrigg comes in.

It might be Short, but it's not a race for novices. After
a mad sprint from the park, and a few metres on the road,

82

the climbing starts at once from the cattle grid, on tarmac initially, and relentlessly steep in the early stages. The route is partly marked though competitors really need to have hill-running experience and must carry a basic minimum of survival kit. There's one checkpoint, staffed by a marshal at the summit, and then it's a descender's dream of a downhill run, on a path that's become established as the shortest and fastest route.

I'm proud to say that Loughrigg marked my farewell to fell racing! Running ever more slowly with age and injuries, I was very conscious that the summit marshals were waiting for me on a cold and maybe wet fell-top. When we set off from the park, I found myself adrift from the rest of the field in a very short time, so it didn't feel as though I was competing against anybody. And then, after finishing almost last in 2019 and scraping home in just under the hour, it was time to offer my services as a volunteer.

Ben Abdelnoor, race organiser for ten years, recalls that he once ran a sub-30 minute race. He's still a very competent runner, with an honourable history, including competing for England in the world long distance championships. He's won the Lakeland 50, Great Lakes, Borrowdale, Fairfield, and Three Shires races, took first place on two occasions at Ennerdale, and had three victories at the Langdale and Wasdale races. He has worked with the juniors in the Ambleside club, and he loves running over Loughrigg. "It's a great training ground, it has everything."

Ben's pleased that the race has stayed low-key, only once

attracting more than 200 runners, and is an inexpensive and friendly event, ideal for those attempting their first fell race. Entry in 2024 cost just £5 and there's always a long and fun prize list, usually including Easter eggs and beer. Cheaper still was the revived Loughrigg-Silver How race which came back onto the calendar early in 2023. "It's £2 to enter, there's no prizes, no technology, old school clipboards for the results." This was recently restored by Ben and his Ambleside AC clubmate Dan Duxbury, though Jim Tyson recalls that the Badger Bar Blast was a Loughrigg-Silver How variant for a couple of years, run from the Rydal side of Loughrigg, up past Rydal Cave visiting the summits of both fells. Silver How, a lovely name for a lovely hill, separated from Loughrigg by the steep tarmac road at Red Bank, overlooks Grasmere. They are perfect companions.

Ben's clubmate Paul Tierney is now the Loughrigg race organiser. But before he stepped down, Ben had to deal with a cruel emergency. In 2017 Stephen Owen, a member of the Penrith-based club Eden Runners, died during the race when he suffered a cardiac arrest from an unknown heart condition. Fellow runners, off-duty medics and volunteers from Langdale Ambleside Mountain Rescue tried unsuccessfully to revive him. The Great North Air Ambulance Service also attended.

Stephen, a Scot with a Welsh name, worked for the Cumbria Wildlife Trust as a reserve and training officer at Eycott Hill nature reserve, having previously worked for the RSPB in Scotland. His partner, Katie Milburn, and friends from Eden Runners subsequently ran the Bob Graham

Round as a relay team, to raise awareness and life-saving funds for the charity Cardiac Risk in the Young. The BG is a 66 mile, 42-summits mountain challenge which runners aim to complete within 24 hours; they finished the route in 22 hours and 28 minutes. Ben ran leg 3 with Eden Runners' Jack Eyre and Scott Morely. Stephen's friends said at the time: "He died surrounded by his friends, and doing what he loved. He was stolen from his love of fell running too soon and was consequently unable to fulfill the mountain running dreams and ambitions he held."

There are other fell races, and trail races, and endurance events for ultra runners ('ultra' loosely meaning anything beyond the marathon distance of 26 miles) all using Loughrigg on their routes. What's the difference? 'Fell' is a term mainly used in the Lake District to describe mountains or high moorland, and the sport of fell-running originated with the guides' and shepherds' races traditionally held alongside wrestling and other sports at the annual games events in Lakeland valleys. Today, the major and most historic remaining of these is Ambleside Sports, always held on the last Thursday in July and featuring both a 'medium' nine-mile distance fell race around the eight summits of the Fairfield Horseshoe, and a series of short and steep guides races for juniors and seniors. The term 'guides' still applies, a link with the sport's history.

So fell-running has been taking place in the UK for many years with the Fell Runners' Association set up in the 1970s to oversee the sport. Races are generally organised by members of local running clubs, with short, medium and long distances, and graded categories depending on the amount of ascent. Runners are expected, mostly, to know where they're going, and navigational skills are needed for all but the shortest races. Entry fees are low, prizes often donated by the local community. Kevan Shand's races in Lancashire used to feature a stack of loo rolls or a year's supply of dog food among the prizes. I once came second at the Gunson Knott race at Stool End farm in Langdale and won a box of bath cubes.

Trail running is a relatively new sport, with roots in America and Europe, which has developed in popularity in the UK over the past 20 years. The terrain will be easier underfoot, following recognised paths, often waymarked, and elevations are less steep. The Lakeland Trails Series, founded by Graham Patten, began in 2006 and now attracts more than 10,000 runners each season. There's likely to be plenty of entertainment and stalls at the start and finish arena, with competitors and spectators treating a trail race as a family day out. Entry fees are usually considerably higher than for fell races; races may well be sponsored by sports firms such as the shoe brand INOV8.

Lakeland Trails, celebrating their 20th anniversary in 2024, promise to "bring you some of the most inspiring trail running events in the UK, all held within the spectacular landscape of the Lake District National Park. Designed for all ages and abilities, our trail courses range from 5k, 10k and 14-18k, through to half and full marathon, then up to Ultra marathon distance. Each provide well marked and marshalled journeys along environmentally sustainable bridleways and footpaths that take in some of the most incredible countryside in Britain. Not only this, a carnival atmosphere is guaranteed for both spectators and competitors, with live music, race commentary, food and drink all available at the start and finish."

Their Ambleside event, the Trail Ultra in July, which takes in a path over the shoulder of Loughrigg, includes races at the distances of 100k, 55k, 23k, and 14k. The 55k route includes three mountain passes, with 7,000-ft ascent along with five well-stocked feed stations. The 100k route adds in an extra three passes, 3500 ft more climbing and three feed stations. The 23k and 14k routes share some of the final sections of the Ultra courses.

Adding to the confusion, also in July are the Montane-sponsored Lakeland 50 and 100 mile races, and these also go over the shoulder of Loughrigg. The organisers say that the 100-miler "is the most spectacular long distance trail race which has ever taken place within the UK. The circular route encompasses the whole of the Lakeland fells, includes in the region of 6300m of ascent and consists almost entirely of public bridleways and footpaths." The route starts in Coniston and heads south before completing a clockwise loop which takes in the Dunnerdale fells, Eskdale, Wasdale and Buttermere before arriving in Keswick. From here the route heads to Matterdale and continues over to Haweswater before returning via Kentmere, Ambleside and Elterwater to the finish at Coniston.

The route doesn't pass over any of the popular Lakeland summits but goes through valleys, contours fellsides and cuts its own line through the challenging Lakeland topography. The event is continuous in nature, competitors don't have to stop or sleep on the route and the winners are generally expected to finish close to the 20 hour mark. The overall time available for the route is 40 hours so sleep at intermediate checkpoints is possible, but time is not on your side.

The 50-mile race is linear, starting at the northern end of Ullswater in the Dalemain Estate before following the eastern shore-line as far as Howtown, then via the banks of Haweswater to Mardale Head. The route then visits Long Sleddale, Kentmere, Ambleside, Langdale and Tilberthwaite before the final climb and descent to the finish at Coniston.

First staged in 2018 is the Lakeland Five Passes Ultra, another summer event, organised by Ascend Events and starting in Grasmere. This route is 32 miles, and includes 10,000 feet of steep climbing, beginning with the summit of Loughrigg.

Also taking in the shoulder of Loughrigg, that is, the path from Miller Bridge to Skelwith Bridge, is the long-established 24-mile Spring in Lakeland event organised by the Long Distance Walkers Association. The LDWA organises many challenge events and local group social walks; challenge events are normally between 20 and 100 miles and must generally be completed within a defined time limit, and have become popular with runners as well as walkers.

The Grasmere Gallop is another popular trail race using

Loughrigg paths, along the Terrace, which has been operating for almost 40 years. There are now two distances – 10k and 17k – along with a 5.7k fun run, and now that the event has teamed up with the organisers of the OMM (Original Mountain Marathon), there's also a marathon race on the same weekend, which also takes in the summit of Loughrigg.

The relative newcomers to the Loughrigg racing scene were the Ambleside 25k and 50k events organised by Brathay events (who stage the annual Windermere road marathon) in partnership with The Climbing Shop in Ambleside. These, too, took in Loughrigg, but at the end of 2023 the Brathay Trust announced its future cancellation. They said: "Brathay Trust's running events are held to raise funds to support our work with disadvantaged children and young people. It is crucial that our investment of time and resources results in a meaningful financial contribution to our charitable activities and outcomes for young people. The Covid pandemic and subsequent rising costs have had a significant impact on our ability to deliver a successful Ambleside 50k and 25k event. Recovery of entry numbers has been slower than expected and the contribution our events make to support Brathay's mission has significantly reduced. Our foremost responsibility is to deliver the Trust's purpose of improving the life chances of thousands of young people in real need every year. It is with this in mind that we have taken the difficult decision to cancel the Ambleside 50k and 25k events from this point forward and direct our resources to alternative fundraising activities."

But Brathay have launched a virtual 10 race, the Tour of Loughrigg, with a start, finish and checkpoints along the way which are detected by the participant's phone, using the Skamper app. It's a good introduction to the area especially, as the organisers point out, for runners who are coming to the Lakes to train for the Langdale marathon and half marathon. Once your entry has been approved you're ready to run the course, any time you like.

You can use the app's map on your phone to navigate the route. The checkpoints will help keep you on track, with an audible signal when you reach them, so it's far removed from the navigational skills required for fell running. But a delightful route, nevertheless.

There's a fascinating story behind another ultra distance race, The Lap, which also takes in the shoulder of Loughrigg. David Newell organises two versions of this, one in May which goes clockwise and a September race that goes anti-clockwise. David explains: "I started putting the route together as a possible mountain bike race in 2010 when I was organising the Windermere Triathlon. As an event organiser and local mountain biker and racer, I wanted my own MTB race. But as a result of too many gates and stiles on the route I filed the map."

Then in 2012 he was diagnosed with MS after losing the use of his left leg while out for a run in the fells. "Shortly after that I began selling off my events and as a former shop manager in Ambleside, I went back to working in outdoor retail." Then, in January 2019, he came across the map while

Loughrigg Tarn, by William Heaton Cooper. Courtesy Heaton Cooper Studio

Loughrigg Tarn, by Stephen Darbishire

Evening at the summit

Paul Mann, Lord of the manor of Loughrigg.
Photos: Chris Routledge

Alone on the hill. Photo: Becky Heaton Cooper

Looking down on Grasmere. Photo: Julie Coldwell

Ben Abdelnoor. Photo: Stephen Wilson

Log cabin in the woods. Construction and photo: John Hempston

Lily Tarn.
Photo: Julie Coldwell

Grass of Parnassus.
Photo: Rebecca Robinson

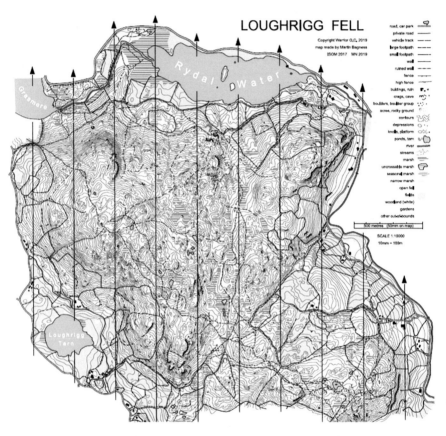

Orienteering map by Martin Bagness

Poetry at the summit: Christopher Wordsworth reading *The World Is Too Much With Us*, with Ava Dove

Dave Peacock and Anna Minh Gammeltoft: engaged at the summit

Cellist Kenneth Wilson plays at Loughrigg summit

Afternoon tea served on the newly rebuilt trig column

Crack in the Woods, a rock climb under Loughrigg

Did she fall or was she pushed? The broken trig column,
February 2023

Pine Rigg in 1964,
and Pine Rigg today

Rydal Cave

Landscape like an overground rabbit warren

Sally Anne Lambert
hula-hooping at the summit

Sketch of the Loughrigg
owl by Liz Wakelin

The Shipman family at their memorial bench near Todd Crag.
Photo: Steve Shipman

The author at the old trig column

Sheep above a small quarry on Loughrigg. Linda Ryle, 1997, oil on canvas

Reading 'The White Goddess' Windermere, 1986. Julian Cooper, oil on canvas

Looking north. Photo: Julie Coldwell

Under Loughrigg after the storm, from *Indeterminate Land* by
Chris Routledge

Antonia Fan descending in the Loughrigg fell race. Photo: Steve Ashworth

Runners on The Lap descending from the fell gate. Photo: Jumpy James

clearing out some old event paperwork. "I immediately saw it as an ultra marathon, and decided to make a comeback. Ultra marathons were few and far between in the UK, apart from a few mountain marathon events and challenges like The Three Peaks race that I used to take part in. By April 2019 I had a website built, online entries open and social media started. I designed the route anticlockwise as I felt this way around was harder, and the first event took place on the second Saturday in September 2019 with 135 runners."

Then came the pandemic and lockdown. "I didn't automatically cancel the event in 2020, but decided to hang in there and see what happened. I did however launch the anticlockwise version for May 2021 just in case September 2020 had to be cancelled. On the second Saturday in September 2020 the event took place with 200 runners, and May 2021 sold out with 300 runners. Both events have sold out faster and faster each year since. We have a team of 50 local people working on event weekend and are one of only a handful of events in the country that actually pay everyone on the team, as I refuse to exploit people's good will to volunteer."

Mike Troup, a retired doctor, still takes part in fell races, but with free time during the day he's out on Loughrigg as often as possible. In 2023, he reckons, he ran up there 113 times, but hardly ever straight up and down the race route. Mike likes to meander.

"My favourite ascent is via Fishgarths Wood, but I also go up directly from Clappersgate, via Fox Ghyll, through Deerbolts wood and up the steps, up behind the caves, up the steps overlooking Loughrigg Tarn, and up the (Silver How) race route from High Close. I rarely go up the road from Miller Bridge – that's a dull ascent. And along Loughrigg Terrace is a bit too popular – and rough, for that matter – to be enjoyable. Highlights? The top, of course, and then Todd Crag, Lily Tarn, Ivy Crag, the views on the descent to High Close: there's so much!"

Some good paths become blocked when the bracken is at its worst, says Mike. And then, after all the climbing, is the joy of running back down. The enthusiasm in his voice is clear: "A descent that's too good not to mention is the one that's been used in the junior races. It starts at the top gate where the main track goes down past the old golf club. Don't go down through the gate, but, instead, go right along the wall, so the wall is on your left. It goes up a bit, levels off, then down and up on grass to a wooden stile. Cross the stile and follow the wall around to the left and just keep going next to the wall; another wooden stile, along a rather boggy bit, and you join the path descending from the kissing gate from Lily Tarn leading to the little wooden bridge. Descend, cross the bridge, and join the main track towards Miller Bridge and Rydal Park. A lovely run that is almost always solitary, though unfortunately not so much fun when the bracken is at its worst."

Mike knows it all intimately: "The path up or down between the little wooden bridge and the kissing gate is a good one in either direction. In ascent in particular it is better than the dull track going up past the old golf club. The almost level track going past Loughrigg Tarn is a good leg stretcher, and it can of course be continued all the way to High Close by joining the minor road. A good runnable uphill is through Deerbolts Woods; better still, start at the top of Loughrigg Terrace, go down through the woods, along Grasmere shore, along the river to White Moss, cross the bridge, come back the other side of the river, across the shore again, and back up through the woods – and finally, of course, up the steps to the top."

He doesn't have to stop and think about any of these route descriptions. It's his home turf, his patch, and he loves it. He sees Loughrigg wildlife, too, deer in Fishgarths and Deerbolts woods, snakes near the top of Todd Crag.

There were no races during the pandemic lockdown, of course, but enterprising runners created challenges which individuals could do at any time. There were the orienteering routes set up by Martin Bagness and John Gomersall, mentioned earlier, and it was John who has keen memories of another challenge, the The Kong Buff trail. This was one of a number of courses set up in different parts of the Lake District by Kong Running, who are race organisers and have a running shop in Keswick. This one started at Pelter Bridge near Rydal, and the aim was to follow 'clues' to find a buff or a chocolate. It was said to take a couple of hours, and that the navigation was 'easy'. Says John: "Always up for a bit of a challenge and I enjoy the orienteering style running, so this trail was for me. Two hours and six miles was about right for me at my age (he's over 70) although 2000ft of climbing might slow me down."

On day one he reached the third checkpoint after running for two hours. Day two presented some unexpected challenges: "After a run out from Ambleside towards the bridge I was faced with flooding and having to wade through water up to my mid thighs to access the marker. Thankfully the next marker was uphill and was exactly where I predicted. After another major climb, I then spent 15 minutes visiting all the small puddles near the summit, before eventually finding the marker at a puddle just below the summit." Soon after that he gave up for the day, too cold and wet to continue.

On day three (remember, this was supposed to take two HOURS) John decided to double check that he had read descriptions and grid references correctly. After much running around, inside and outside Rydal Cave, and revisiting all the little crag tops he'd been to on the second day, he returned to the cave entrance and "thought like a fell runner and started visiting every crag top within 100 metres. Eventually I struck lucky."

But he still couldn't find the locations for the return to Pelter Bridge, so returned for a fourth day. "After checking the grid reference on a proper map (rather than GPS) and wearing my reading glasses, I realised my mistake and knew where to look. The moral of this story, well three actually: Don't trust electronic devices, think like a fell runner, carry reading glasses." But the route, and Loughrigg, had given him an entertaining four days. Small mountain, maybe, but a complex one.

It's also the final summit on a personal challenge event which was established by Elterwater Independent Hostel some years ago. It's called 23 Before Tea and was the South Lakes' answer to a run from Keswick, George Fisher's Tea Round, a circuit of all the fell tops you can see from the cafe at the top of Fisher's outdoor shop. What can we do here, the hostel team asked, just after local lad Paul Tierney had set a new record for running *all* the Wainwrights.*

I had a large-scale map on my wall at home of Paul's route, based on the line used previously by Steve Birkinshaw, because I'd been helping with the organisation of his adventure. I took a photo with the hostel directly in the centre, and homing in till actual fell tops were visible, I counted 23 summits within that square. The name, 23 Before Tea, came from a friend who had been in the Lakes helping with a Bob Graham attempt.

So we had a name and a list of mountains, and Adrian Thomas, whose folks own the hostel, bravely set out to try and cover them all – and be home in time for tea. It was a challenge too far; these were random mountain tops, with far too much descent to the valley bottom and re-ascent. But the fellrunning community started to chatter about it, and when lockdown put paid to actual peak-bagging, an enterprising young man, Dave Cumins, known to all as Little Dave, looked more seriously at the map. From his home in Brighton, 342 miles away, he created a route linking 23 summits which still had Elterwater at its heart.

When travel restrictions were lifted, he headed north to try it, and the challenge took off. Since then the route has been streamlined, and the record time lowered, by a succession of very talented distance runners. At the time of writing, it was held by Gavin Dale, an Ambleside runner who has tackled the route three times, and raced round in five hours 47 minutes in November 2023.

Any 23 Wainwrights will do, but the currently-recognised fastest route is as follows, starting and finishing at the hostel gate: Silver How, Blea Rigg, Pavey Ark, Harrison Stickle, Loft Crag, Pike of Stickle, Thunacar Knott, High Raise, Sergeant Man, Tarn Crag, Calf Crag, Gibson Knott, Helm Crag, Nab Scar, Heron Pike, Stone Arthur, Great Rigg, Fairfield, Hart Crag, Dove Crag, High Pike, Low Pike and Loughrigg.

And in every incarnation since the beginning, Loughrigg has been the final fell. It's possible to stand outside the hostel in the dark (yes, I've been there several times!) and watch for head torches coming down off my small mountain.

*Paul Tierney went on to set a new Wainwrights record, involving 320 miles (515 km) and 118,000 ft (36,000m) of ascent, of six days six hours and four minutes.

The first recorded continuous round of all 214 Wainwrights was completed by Alan Heaton between 29 June and 8 July 1985 starting and finishing at Keswick Moot Hall in 9 days and 16 hours. Joss Naylor completed the round in 7 days in 1986 and held the record until 20 June 2014 when Steve Birkinshaw lowered it to 6 days and 13 hours. Following on from Paul's run, in 2021 Sabrina

Verjee ran round in 5 days 23 hours 49, and this time was beaten by John Kelly, a data scientist from Tennessee, in 2022 who ran the route in 5 days, 12 hours and 14 minutes.

Soundtrack: Keep on running, The Spencer Davis Group

CHAPTER SIX

A TALE OF TWO TARNS

How many tarns are there on Loughrigg, I once asked map-maker Martin Bagness. Well, he said, it depends what you mean by a tarn. And sure enough if you study his map, the most detailed piece of cartography ever devoted to Loughrigg Fell, there's a great many patches of blue, large and small. Some are marshes and bogs, some are occasional puddles, little more than dewponds, Wainwright calls them, which might dry up and disappear in a hot summer.

But there are two of significance, two small bodies of water which are each exquisitely lovely, very different from one another in size and character, and each loved with a passion by many admirers. Loughrigg Tarn is the bigger jewel, Lily Tarn is the baby sister, in a most beautiful setting, a place of utter peace and tranquility, seldom busy with walkers.

She's at 200m (655 feet), lying in a swampy hollow to the east of Todd Crag, that wonderful outcrop of Loughrigg which is a magnificent place from which to view the whole of Windermere. But Lily Tarn is secretive and hidden. So many paths cross this part of the fell, and if you lose concentration for just a moment, Lily Tarn has disappeared, moved by fairy folk perhaps. There's a way up through Fishgarths wood above Clappersgate, but most walkers take the enchanting path that leaves the main climb up Loughrigg Brow at a sharp bend in the track. Climb over a stone stile in the wall, head a short way through dark woodland and fallen trees, and then over a little wooden footbridge into a magical world.

Visitors' first memories of Lily Tarn are interesting. People have got confused, uncertain if not downright lost, and I can say this with authority, for I 'lost' Lily Tarn several times when I first started climbing Loughrigg regularly. Who's moved it, again, I'd mutter. In mist she's even more beguiling.

Lily is tiny, roughly 63 x 53m (205 x 170 feet), covering an area of just 0.23 hectares and at her deepest only three feet. The eponymous lilies are there from late spring, though under siege from a bigger plant, and in the middle is a tiny island, only a few metres in extent. Wainwright, writing in 1958, noted that "some quiet humorist has erected a cairn on it" but the cairn went a long time ago. There was a slender, short silver birch tree which fell over a few years ago; a replacement was planted shortly afterwards by Ben Abdelnoor in what he calls a "bit of guerilla gardening". One summer evening he waded, part swimming, with a trug containing the sapling and a spade. "I lost a sock on the way down (I'd taken my socks and shoes off for the dip) but found it in the bracken a few weeks later."

In *Sketching a Year in Lakeland* Liz Wakelin describes a visit to Lily Tarn when she was suffering cabin fever after several days of rain: "At the tarn the surface rippled silver and black and the bogbean danced in the wind. In summer there will be lilies blooming but in May it is the delicate pink and white flowers of the bogbean that hold sway. In good conditions the views from this outlier of Loughrigg Fell are superb, but the weather was worsening and the world turning black with rain so I tightened my hood and hurried down feeling much better for the fresh air."

Ah, the bogbean. I'm on the side of those who believe this is a bully of a plant, forcing the water lilies out of their best populated corner of the tarn. Others love the bogbean's flowers, and feel that the natural order should be allowed to rule. Naturalist Pete Martin finds the bogbean more interesting, "probably because I knew the latter (Nymphaea alba) when I was a kid but didn't know the former (Menyanthes trifoliata).

"As far as I am aware they are both native plants, so neither is a 'beastly invader'; both are beautiful things, and beauty is in the eye of the beholder. I would argue that both are intrinsically valuable as individual species.

"Is Lily Tarn natural, or made by peat cutting in past centuries? All lakes are temporary features. Did the plants in question get there naturally… or were they put there by folk?

"I don't know of any direct competition between the two plants. Any change in relative abundance is probably due to what's going on around and in the tarn. Things might be happening to one or the other or both or neither. Correlation is not necessarily causation. I think the white water lily needs deeper water (though I might be wrong); bogbean can certainly grow in less deep areas and smaller ponds, so any

apparent increase in bogbean/ decrease in water lily may be
a response to a decrease in water depth an increase in silt/
increased drying out due to warmer summers/ drier springs.

"What I do know is that the water lobelia (Lobelia
dortmanna) is highly sensitive, and while it used to be present
in Lily Tarn, I haven't seen it there in recent years. Which is a
real shame as it's a beautiful thing."

The lilies win hands down for me, and if it came to a
battle for survival, who would want to visit Bogbean Tarn?
But let's move on, to a lovely lyrical account of a cold winter's
day back in 2009, from the blog of nature writer Jan Wiltshire
(www.cumbrianaturally.co.uk)

A prolonged period of Arctic weather and the coldest winter
of the decade, with skaters and children tempted onto frozen
lakes and tarns.

We set out from Ambleside, earth hard as iron, and came
upon a frozen Lily Tarn scattered with chunks of ice. Bracken
glowed deep and warm, though visibility was poor with a low
cloud base and high humidity. Above Ivy Crag, water droplets
had rimed seed-heads and tussocks of tall grasses waved white
in the chilly wind. Higher still, en route for the trig point on
Loughrigg Fell, bracken fronds were rimed to windward in
a fretwork of ice, the wondrous creation of days and nights
of freezing fog. Undulating paths wound about knolls and
an ice-mantle overspread saturated ground, habitat of bog
asphodel and cross-leaved heath.

A descent by dark juniper gullies overhung with outcropping

rock. In the gloom of an early afternoon the River Rothay ran black as ink, with purple alder catkins and old cones. Below Nab Scar, we sat looking across Rydal Water toward Loughrigg, now lost in mist and murk.

Toward Rydal Hall, someone on a quad bike dragged a limb of rhododendron, a shuddering screen of foliage. Ancient trees in Rydal Park were embossed with great burrs. A fire blazed where five years ago an oak had fallen and now, threatening to topple onto the footpath, it was being sawn up. There was a row of cut logs and the woodcutter had stacked branches and kindling against the huge stump of the oak and fired it to reduce its size before he shifted it. A shower of sparks, and a red-hot glow at the heart of the fire was focal point in the gloom and chill of a January afternoon.

Another blogger, who writes as Forest 86, describes an attempt to swim here:

I decided to park in Clappersgate and make my way up to Lily Tarn on the south eastern edge of Loughrigg. The path up is lovely, quite steep but with great views over to Windermere. Lily Tarn is very picturesque, a small tarn with one tiny island in the middle supporting a small shrub and a single silver birch tree. It was a bit cloudy and grey, but still fairly warm and I was hopeful that the water wouldn't be too cold! There were a few dragonflies around at the far side as I got into the water, something I've seen quite a lot on my swims, but for the first time I managed to get a reasonable photo of one. The water was very, very shallow and I soon realised that this was going to be another tarn where it was more a case of dragging myself through mud than of swimming! As I stirred up the layers of sediment on the bottom the familiar smell of the disturbed gas rose up to accompany me as the mud itself found ways to cling to every part of my body. I was worried for a moment, remembering that I was meant to be going for lunch after this and remembering Kelly Hall Tarn where I got out covered in a thick layer of mud which it took quite a lot of determined excavations to remove. Luckily, though, the tarn got slightly deeper (by which I mean it probably would've come slightly above my knees if I'd stood up) and the bottom got a bit stonier so the water was clearer. I managed to get an underwater picture where you can actually see my face and to wash off the majority of the mud. Despite the battle with the sediment this was an enjoyable swim although I wouldn't recommend it as a swimming spot unless you are a pixie. There is, however, a well-placed bench on the shore, so it would be a lovely place to sit and enjoy the view.

The bench is a simple, backless wooden seat. Some years ago, after heavy snowfall, I walked up there with Sarah Jones and her son Tom. We built a very rudimentary snowman sitting on the bench. Later that day another friend, Britta Sendlhofer, posted a photo on facebook. She had been to Lily Tarn afterwards and, not knowing who had created the primitive original, set about adding some delightful features... eyes, nose, mouth, proper feet at the end of his legs, and a hat, of course. This, it seemed, was art in the landscape at its best.

And so to Loughrigg Tarn, something of a tautology since Loughrigg means "ridge above the lough (lake)" (Diana Whaley, *A Dictionary of Lakeland Place-Names,*) and "tarn" is also the name of a body of water. William Wordsworth, in his *Guide to the Lakes* described Loughrigg Tarn as "the most beautiful example of the class of miniature lakes".

> It has a margin of green firm meadows, of rocks, and rocky woods, a few reeds here, a little company of waterlilies there, with beds of gravel or stone beyond; a tiny stream issuing neither briskly nor sluggishly out of it; but its feeding rills, from the shortness of their course, so small as to be scarcely visible. Five or six cottages are reflected in its peaceful bosom; rocky and barren steeps rise up above the hanging enclosures; and the solemn pikes at Langdale overlook, from a distance, the low cultivated ridge of land that forms the northern boundary of this small, quiet and fertile domain.

In his poem 'Epistle to George Howard Beaumont' in 1811, he wrote that Loughrigg is "as round and clear and bright as heaven" and he continued:

> And soon approach Diana's Looking-glass!
> To Loughrigg-tarn, round clear and bright as heaven,
> Such name Italian fancy would have given,
>   ... when an opening in the road
> Stopped me at once by charm of what it showed,
> The encircling region vividly exprest
> Within the mirror's depth, a world at rest

Diana's Looking Glass was also a 'found-footage' film of 1996 in which the directors Yervant Gianikian and Angela Ricci Lucchi recall the genealogy of imperial fantasies. In 1927, Mussolini had given the order to drain Lake Nemi to salvage the remains of two magnificent ships from Emperor Caligula, reviver of the Diana myth.

Loughrigg Tarn, while considerably bigger than Lily, is still a small body of water, almost circular in form, 94 metres (308ft) above sea level and has a shallow basin of 10m (32ft) at the northern shore, still a lot deeper than Lily. It's surrounded by grassland, scattered woodland and wetland areas which slope gently towards the shoreline, and sits in an elevated position close to the entrance of Great Langdale. It's peacefully out of sight to any passers-by unless they happen to be walking on this side of the fell.

The tarn and the surrounding land of the High Close estate, once a hamlet of cottages, was originally owned by the Benson family, and then later the Balme family who extended and refurbished the farmhouse between 1866-76. Its 537 acres have been under the care of the National Trust since 1952. Across the narrow road, surrounded by the High Close arboretum, is the YHA hostel.

The surroundings are exquisite, the backdrop stunning, with the sharp outline of the Langdale Pikes. The Balme family were responsible for planting many of the trees along the bridleway, which was once part of their private driveway. But there's one notable tree that William Heaton Cooper described, "an oak tree was pollarded many years ago, and out of its hearts have sprouted a yew, a holly, a rowan and a silver birch."

Loughrigg Tarn is the result of glacial action, with the ice that excavated this depression coming from Grasmere to the north. It moved over the col of Red Bank, the lowest section between Loughrigg Fell and Silver How in a south-easterly direction into Great Langdale. This action is known as diffluence where one tongue of ice effectively cuts across the boundary of two catchment areas, the result of which created the elevated basin of Loughrigg Tarn we see today (*TheEnglishLakes.uk.*)

Wainwright describes the tarn in *The Central Fells,* on the ascent of Loughrigg from Skelwith Bridge. "Loughrigg Tarn is one of the most secluded of tarns and rarely visible from the fells. It is excellently seen from certain points on this walk, however." It's not easily reached by car, with very limited parking above Skelwith Bridge, and so the tarn is favoured by walkers, runners and swimmers who love that sense of seclusion. Campers too, for just beyond the south eastern shore is the delightful Tarn Foot Farm campsite. It's a traditional site, with a couple of toilets and a tap in the farmyard, no fancy showers, no barbecue pits, no on-site bar or children's 'play area', though my children played here very happily when they were young. As one reviewer wrote: "It's not a site if you like 'glamping', but this is camping as it should be. Cheap and basic, in a beautiful place, surrounded by nature."

There's also plenty of wildlife that call this place home, including minnow, pike, perch, ducks, moorhens and whooper swans, along with the species known as the wild swimmer. This must be one of the loveliest places to swim in the Lake District where the water is relatively warm as no major rivers feed into it. Most days, from April through till October, you'll find Sarah Knight swimming here, or just sitting by the water and looking out across to the surrounding hills. Sarah's a swimming professional, helping to run guided swims and open water swimming courses in the many lakes and tarns of the Lake District.

But the daily visit to Loughrigg Tarn, by bicycle, is what she does before or after work. It's a very special place, she says. There's the scenery, to start with. "There are many lovely tarns but very few that have the combination of the water lilies and the impressive mountain setting here." Then there's the wildlife. "There are great crested grebes that nest here every year, you can swim past the nest and see them feeding their chicks right in front of you. There are herons, swans, geese and ducks that come to be fed daily, if you are very lucky the glimpse of an occasional kingfisher and, in spring, the lambs."

And there's an interesting dichotomy, because while Sarah loves the solitude of the tarn, its accessibility while being off the busy beaten tracks, it can also be a very sociable place to swim. "If I go in the early morning, I'm often lucky enough to have the place all to myself. But at other times of the day, this is where the locals and wise visitors come to swim, so there is usually someone to talk to. They will be like-minded people who come regularly, many who have visited the tarn over the years and are always drawn back. It's an interesting combination, and another reason why Loughrigg Tarn is such a special place."

Sarah trained and worked as a teacher, then worked for Impact International, the Ambleside-based globally-recognised company that specialises in leadership and team development, change management and well-being at work. It was here that she met Pete Kelly, delivering a bespoke guided swimming session. She now works for his Swim the Lakes business as a swim guide and has also worked in his shop selling kit for open water swimmers. Their Introduction to Open Water courses are held mostly in Windermere, and the lake, like others, has become very busy in recent times with boat users, paddle-boarders and kayakers, says Sarah.

Loughrigg Tarn, by contrast, is private land owned by the National Trust, who in recent years have stopped the use of boats, paddle boards and kayaks, to protect the habitats and wildlife there. Access is still permitted to walkers and swimmers who can enjoy the beauty and peacefulness of this secluded environment. "You can swim there any time of the day and it has a really calming effect. It's possible to get away from the crowds, at least during the week, and the Tarn gives you a sense of well-being that really is unique."

Edna Garlick knows Loughrigg Tarn better than most. For 53 years she lived at Crag Head, a low two-storey National Trust cottage looking out across the water, and with the summit of Little Loughrigg behind the house. Now widowed, and living near the centre of Ambleside, Edna's memories are sharp, full of tales of her three lively sons, and occasional sadness. She witnessed tragedy on at least two occasions, as she will recall.

She and her husband Bill moved to the Lakes in 1968 when he took a job with the National Trust. Edna, orginally from very urban Stockport, had moved with Bill when work took him south to Aylesbury. "But I didn't like living in the south, and when he said, how about moving to the Lake District, I was happy to give it a go." She had to be interviewed by Bill's employers, who needed to be sure that a wife and mother, whose youngest son was just 18 months old, would be able to cope with living in a remote cottage with no bathroom, no hot water, and an earth closet outside instead of a toilet. "I never looked back," she says. "I was made of tough stuff. The toilet was at the end of the garden, with a gap at the top of the door. The view from the loo was something special. We had a bathroom and toilet installed after about six months."

The children went to school at Skelwith, in the building that is now the village hall, and a local farmer would collect them each morning and drive them there with his own grandchildren. After school her three boys had the freedom of the fell and the tarn, to play and to fish. "The boys had no parameters, they could play wherever they wanted." Once they caught a huge pike, she remembers, but it was mostly perch and roach, and occasionally eels "that had come all the way from the Sargasso Sea." Every year, it seems, eels leave European rivers to travel in an epic migration to the Sargasso Sea in the North Atlantic to breed for a single time, then die.

Badgers chewed through the television cable that ran the length of the garden, and there was a constant battle to keep sheep away from the plants. The delivery driver who brought groceries from the Co-op store at Chapel Stile always locked his van door after a fox had crept in and stolen all the bacon. Once Edna watched as a stoat carried a fully-grown rabbit into the eaves of her house to feed its family. "We had heard scrabbling and scratching and didn't know what it was. Eventually we were lucky enough to be in the garden when they all scrambled down the ivy and away they went."

There was a private water supply from a spring, and once, when Edna called a plumber as the tap seemed to be blocked, a long white frog came out. "We just put it in the garden and away it hopped." During times of drought she and Bill would check the water tank daily to see how much water was left "and then we acted accordingly, which meant no washing."

But two of her sharpest memories are of tragedy. "I was at home one day with the children when they were little, and a girl came to the door shouting for help, that her mum and a friend were in the tarn. The man had gone through the ice; he had skates on. The girl said that she too had fallen into the water but her mum had managed to push her out. I ran down to the edge and saw there was no way I could go on that ice, so I ran back to the house and cut down the washing line. I threw it to the woman, and she grabbed it first time, and I managed to pull her out." But the man had drowned. "The next day the National Trust gave Bill the day off, to take me out of the way while they dragged the tarn to get his body out."

The other death she witnessed happened when she was at home watching the wedding of Prince Charles and Lady Diana Spencer on TV. "There was a cry for help outside. A man who had been swimming with his son had drowned in the tarn. That's what I will always remember about the royal wedding." Previously, before Edna moved to Loughrigg, a 12-year-old boy had drowned in the tarn while on a school trip. A memorial cross near the shore of the tarn commemorates the accident.

But let's end this chapter on a note of romance, with some words from the artist Stephen J. Darbishire RBA who lives with his wife and family in a 17th century farmhouse hidden in the mountains not far from here. The love of his surroundings comes to life through his paintings. The interiors of cottages and farmhouses, sunlight pouring in through windows, fires burning in open hearths, tables laid for afternoon tea (Kerry, his wife, and a fine poet, loves to cook), vases of flowers from the hedgerows and gardens; the celebration of the seasons. Sometimes he also paints love stories.

> Loughrigg Tarn is indeed a looking glass – Diana's, as Wordsworth recalled it, round, clear and bright as heaven. And to us, it still is a tarn of reflection – our courting days. In summer after work, we'd walk up the steep road by Mill Brow farm, trying to catch the last rays of sun lowering

behind the Langdale Pikes. There was always a kerfuffle of barking dogs as we walked past Harry Wilson's farm, busy and beautiful as it had been for generations. This was the late 1960s before Tarn Foot campsite became popular. Two friends lived in a caravan behind a cottage. They made it their home for years. But then, with no one else around, from the lane that circles the tarn, down the field we'd run from the heat of the day, each of us wanting to be first in. The pleasure of cooling down, ruffling the calm surface, swimming as if to steal the perfect reflection of the Langdale Pikes.

Soundtrack: Pictures of Lily, The Who

CHAPTER SEVEN

TRIANGULATION

It was April the First, so a good day to do something a
bit wacky, which is how Sally Anne and I came to be
hula-hooping by the trig point on Loughrigg. I have form
around April Fool's day. Some years ago, helping to promote
a friend's sports coaching business, we decided to create a
new race from Ambleside to the top of Wansfell and back on
April 1. The same route as the winter event, only this one was
to be for pairs. And knowing there were sometimes difficulties
(in mountain marathons and fell relays) persuading pairs of
runners to stay together through checkpoints, we announced
that our pairs would be tied together. The Wansfell Two-Step
would be a three-legged race. We staged a publicity shot
featuring six feet six inches tall Wayne Singleton, athletics
coach and founder of Jogging Pals, and just over five feet high
ultra-runner Jo Kilkenny. The fact that the inaugural event
was cancelled because of lockdown added to the 'news' value,
and we made people smile when humour was in short supply.

This time it wasn't an April fool joke, strictly, just an
excuse to raise some money for the Fix the Fells team on
behalf of Elterwater Independent Hostel where I was doing

some work. Fix the Fells is a team of skilled rangers and volunteers who repair and maintain the mountain paths in the Lake District with funding from donations and partners. A combination of millions of pairs of walking boots, the weather, and the gradient means erosion is a constant problem; their path work reduces erosion scars and also helps protect the ecology and archaeological heritage of the landscape.

No skill in those departments, but hula-hooping is one of the few things I'm really good at. I used to be QUITE good at fell-running, but apart from the knack of making excellent compost, this is the one area where I excel. It's pure chance, I'm sure; I just know how to rock backwards and forwards for a long time and even, during lockdown, came close to winning a street competition when we decided to test who could keep hooping the longest. I was in danger of defeating the only remaining challenger, an eight-year-old schoolgirl, so I bowed out deliberately and gracefully into second place.

On this April day we took plenty of food and drink and lots of extra layers, and the best hoop, and walked up to the summit the 'short' way, from the back of the High Close arboretum, and spent the day asking walkers if they would like to have a go. We got some great photos and video footage, met some delightful ramblers, and raised a tidy sum; pre-pandemic, folk still had cash in their pockets when they went for a walk.

It was the first time I'd spent more than a few minutes by the trig column, though I would always touch the top, my own talisman. Maybe once or twice if no one was around,

I might give it a hug. During the year that I first made 50 ascents of Loughrigg, there was one December day when I had to crawl on hands and knees from the top of the steps to the trig, so fierce was the wind. But a summit attempt doesn't count unless you really reach the top.

Often, though, there were clear days and good views, pivoting round to count the lakes: Grasmere, Windermere, Elterwater, Esthwaite Water, and the tiny corner of Thirlmere. Not Rydal Water; you can't see her from the summit. I loved talking to people at the top, folk who had come from all over the world, some making repeat visits, some on their first trip to the Lake District. Tiny people in backpacks, solo hikers with cameras whose body language said, go away, I'm concentrating. People with dogs; Liz Wakelin met a cat called Mr Mittens who had walked to the summit with his 'servants', two young women who had given up their jobs to travel in a camper van for a while. He has his own Instagram account, Mr Mittens' Adventures. If he gets tired they have a backpack to carry him but he generally walks everywhere. He had a harness and a lead for moments when he needed to be close by.

Usually I'd ask if walkers were on holiday and, if so, where were they from, and that would lead to, "Oh lovely, I've done Hull/Preston/Skipton/Coventry parkrun" and sometimes they, too, would be parkrunners and we would chat for a while. Wayne Singleton, who witnessed a few of these conversations, claims that my record for introducing the word 'parkrun' was 18 seconds.

One night I slept out at the summit, a moody evening in July when I borrowed a tiny mountain tent, and climbed the path from behind High Close, what Becky Heaton Cooper's children call Bag End ("they are obsessed with the Shire") with a flask of tea for the morning, and a small flask of whisky for supper. There's a perfect flat space just below the trig on the north side, and that's where I pitched camp. Others had the same idea that evening, but I'd grabbed the best location and they had to camp further away. The dawn was disappointing, grey and misty, but it was a lovely experience just to be there.

Wainwright was enchanted by the top of Loughrigg, and the trig in particular. He wrote in *The Central Fells*: "Three eminences rise close together above the undulating top of the fell, and the middle one, slightly higher than the others, bears the main cairn and an Ordnance Survey triangulation column that the surveyors who built it, after building so many, must have voted the most beautifully situated of all." Main cairn? The sketch on Loughrigg page 11 clearly shows a big pile of stones behind the trig, but they were really unnecessary and disappeared many years ago.

The story of the birthday cake tied with a balloon and wedged under a stone beside the trig has already been told, so it's not surprising that I felt hurt and saddened to learn, while away on holiday early in 2023, that the Loughrigg trig column had collapsed. Did it fall or was it pushed? Locals who found it saw that the central, hollow metal tube had clearly corroded, but how had the stonework given way? There was mention of lightning strikes, but there had been no thunderstorms that week. There was talk of vandalism, even of using fireworks to blast the column apart. Whatever the cause, the broken column was a very sad sight.

Trig – triangulation – pillars are the once-useful relics of another age, defiantly upright and proud even though technology has made them redundant. Not every fell or mountain top has one, and sometimes it feels as though summit cairns have been built to make up for the deficit. They are always impressively situated, and on Loughrigg and many others they command outstanding views.

A trig pillar was first used in the retriangulation of the country in April 1936 when a group of surveyors gathered around a white concrete pillar in a field in Cold Ashby near the Northamptonshire, Leicestershire and Warwickshire borders, and began the retriangulation of Britain. Triangulation is a mathematical process that makes accurate map-making possible. In the early 20th century, mapmaking was still based on the Principal Triangulation which was a piecemeal collection of observations taken between 1783 and 1853. The system was starting to collapse and couldn't support the more accurate mapping needed to track the rapid development of Britain after the Great War.

In 1935 the Ordnance Survey, in a project led by Brigadier Martin Hotine, decided to implement a completely new control network for the whole country and, at the same time, unify the mapping from local county projections onto a single national datum, projection and reference system. This led to the OSGB36 datum and The National Grid, both of which are still with us today.

It was Brigadier Hotine, head of the Trigonometrical and Levelling Division at OS – what a title! – who designed the trig pillar that we all recognise today. The brigadier was responsible for the design, planning and implementation of the retriangulation, and he designed the iconic trig pillar to provide a solid base for the theodolites used by the survey teams to improve the accuracy of the readings obtained. The last one came into action in June 1962 when the trig pillar at Thorney Gale, Westmorland, a hamlet north-east of Kirkby Stephen, was used for the final calculation.

The Ordnance Survey have published a blog (https://www.ordnancesurvey.co.uk/blog/trig-pillar-trivia) explaining further. Triangulation works by determining the location of a point by measuring angles to it from known points at either end of a fixed baseline and, in this case, those known points were the 6,500-plus trig pillars erected across the country. In practice, a theodolite would have been secured to the top mounting plate and made level. It would then be directly over the brass bolt underneath the pillar. Angles were then measured from the pillar to other surrounding points.

For the highest accuracy primary points in the retriangulation, many rounds of angles would have been measured with the observations taking several hours. But time and technology have moved to the point where the traditional trig pillar is now obsolete in its original guise. Ordnance Survey now uses the OS Net Network of 110 global navigation satellite system receivers to map accurately to within a few centimetres, in seconds, what previously took hours and days to do.

Not surprisingly, the one on top of Ben Nevis is the highest in the UK, and while trig pillars are often on peaks of hills, the lowest sits at -0.533m below sea level near Ely in Cambridgeshire. The brass fitting on the top of a pillar (three grooves set at 120 degrees apart) is known as a 'Spider'. This is a 'forced centring' device to ensure any survey instrument (such as a theodolite) is centred over the reference mark. The brass loops on the top are so that the instrument can be tied down in windy weather.

Trig pillars are seen as quintessentially British and made it onto Bill Bryson's list of favourite British items in his 2015 book, *The Road to Little Dribbling*. Not in the Lake District though, but in Devon where he confessed to a map-reading failure. "I am not at all sure how a series of triangles gives you a map of Britain – and please don't write to tell me; I'm not saying that I want to know – but somehow it does and that's what matters… I expect there is somewhere in Britain a Trig Society. I also imagine that now I have written this they will ask me to come and speak at their annual meeting. So let me say here that I miss trig points a lot, but not that much."

Once they became redundant there was a swell of interest in adopting trig pillars and an official process was set in place, but the OS no longer keep the records of who owns what. But in that peculiarly British habit of collecting things – from stamps to train spotting – there are thousands of people who 'collect' trig points, and they have their own website, if not a Society, https://trigpointing.uk/. This, the organisers explain, is for those people who are unable to walk past a trigpoint without bagging it. On their pages you will find information about trigpointing, and be able to log your finds. "We have a database containing the locations of most of the trigpoints in Great Britain, but if you find one that we don't know about, please add it to our database."

As a snapshot on the day that I checked the statistics, there were 5836 contributing users, of whom 316 were active (ie, had logged in during the previous 30 days). To date there had been 426,348 total logs, and 362,769 photos of trigs. So by no means a minority interest pastime. Triggers tick things off and create spreadsheets with all the fervour of Wainwright peak-baggers and parkrun tourists. And it was one of their members who kindly told me that the next trig points in each direction from Loughrigg are High Arnside (Black Crag) to the south; Red Screes to the east; High Raise to the west; and Helvellyn to the north.

The summit of Loughrigg, and therefore the trig column, is owned by the Lowther Estate, who own around 90,000 acres of the Lake District National Park. This includes the managed ruin of Lowther Castle and its lovely gardens, near Penrith, and the estate has belonged to the Lowther family, latterly the Earls of Lonsdale, since the Middle Ages. The estate comprises a portfolio of land including forests, farms and cottages, quarries, and common land which includes Great Langdale Commons, Little Langdale

Commons, Easedale, Elterwater, Chapel Stile, and Grasmere and Loughrigg Commons. There's a map showing how much of Loughrigg they own, which is most of it, including Lily Tarn, but not Loughrigg Tarn (National Trust) nor the approach route on the main bridleway from Miller Bridge to the fell gate beyond Pine Rigg.

The estate deals with landscape repairs, along with improving the enjoyment of the Commons for visitors, and works with Natural England to improve various habitats, and the rebuilding of the Loughrigg trig column was their responsibility. But it wasn't a job that could be done in a hurry. As they explained to a number of enquirers, there was no point doing repairs until the risk of frost was past, because the cement wouldn't set.

That made sense but, as the weeks went by, I wasn't the only one to feel saddened by what had happened. I started doing circuitous routes to avoid visiting the summit, and several local people said they were doing likewise. It was May before the column was restored. By then, Steve Tonkin and a group of friends were on the brink of going up Loughrigg with their own tub of cement. Steve's a mountain man, walker, adventurer, wild swimmer, who works for the Lake District Foundation which is the main fundraiser for the Fix the Fells programme. But Andy Whitworth from Lowther, with his colleague Noel Waller (a waller by profession) were there to do the job, to the delight of many people climbing the fell that day. Andy said later: "That was one of the nicest days I have had in the Lakes during my working life. Everyone we met appreciated what we were doing."

Not everyone was pleased with the result. The new column was shorter, as the broken central metal tube was reused, and some thought the finish rougher than they had hoped. Artist Liz Wakelin summed it up. "It's no longer as elegant. Sturdy would be the best way the describe it."

Why did the trig column matter, why did its collapse cause such an emotional response? Pete Martin, who knows the hill intimately, says: "Something that is designed with pure practicality becomes important in people's hearts for different reasons, starting with that triangulation to do the measuring."

Pete has kept correspondence relating to an earlier incident, as I learned now that the trig column had broken back in 2003. In a letter to Pete from the Ordnance Survey in September 2003, they told him that it appeared the Loughrigg column had never been adopted after the OS no longer needed it, "and the adoption scheme itself has been closed for several years now so you won't be able to adopt it." They believed at the time that the landowner was the National Trust and suggest Pete should contact them. "If a pillar was in a dangerous position then we would have to visit it asap. The majority of pillars are not included in our GPS network but there are some which are deemed important because of where they are sited, eg, tops of hills for navigational purposes."

Pete then wrote to the National Trust who told him that they leased much of the common land in the Great Langdale and Grasmere valleys from the Lowther Estates "and this includes Loughrigg fell."

The letter went on: "I must admit that I had not considered the Triangulation Pillar as part of our responsibilities before and I expect that legally it is not. However I appreciate the importance of this particular summit to many people and agree that it would be a shame for the pillar to fall into disrepair... . As we are not really responsible for its maintenance I will ask the Ordnance Survey and other possible interested parties if they could contribute towards any costs that we would face in any repairs."

Finally, in a letter dated February 9, 2004, Pete was told: "I have since consulted with the National Park authority and the Ordnance Survey. I am writing to let you know that the National Trust will repair the Triangulation Pillar as soon as it is possible."

Now, 19 years later, we were about to celebrate the rebuilding of our talisman once again. Chris and Siobhan Routledge, who live at the foot of the hill, went up on the Friday evening with glasses and gin and tonic, and posted a photo on social media: "We note that the new trig column is bar height." Spurred by this, I decided to mark the occasion in a different style. On the Sunday afternoon my sister Sheila and I went up to the top with rucksacks full of scones, jam and cream, and we laid out a china teapot and cups and saucers on the pillar's flat table-top. We then offered afternoon tea to passers by who were bemused, and delighted, in equal measure. "What's it for?" we were asked regularly. "Fun," I said.

A few months earlier, just before Christmas 2022, I'd put out a call on social media for anyone who was free to join me on the summit of Loughrigg for mince pies. Friends responded with typical excuses: office party, Christmas shopping, collecting grandma from the station. So I went alone, with a box of mince pies and a flask of mulled wine and paper cups. I shared this seasonal picnic with some delightful strangers, one of whom said: "You've created a memory for us."

So now that we had the pillar back, perhaps we should create a few more memories? Some time ago I got to know a cellist called Kenneth Wilson. I'm drawn towards eccentrics and their lives, and Kenneth was a feature writer's dream. He decided to cycle from his home near Hadrian's Wall to Rome, carrying his cello on the back of his bicycle, and he hoped to play along the way in exchange for accommodation.

I've become used to talking to Kenneth in unusual places. Our first conversation was when I interviewed him by phone when he was playing his cello on a punt on the river in Cambridge; there was a second phone call when he was playing outside Canterbury Cathedral, and was shortly afterwards invited inside by the bishop to play at the evening service.

That was at the start of his cycling odyssey, but when he came back I interviewed him at his home in a treehouse in rural Cumbria. You should write a book, I said, and now he has. *Highway Cello* is the story of the adventures of this poet, musician, ex-vicar, failed property developer and reformed vegetarian who once ran an India travel company. It's the saga of a preposterously ambitious journey on a fifty-year-old Dawes Galaxy bicycle, with the cello – named Libre – strapped to the back of it.

Kenneth's a busker who found that he'd outgrown all the natural musical places to play in Penrith near his home, and started to dream of playing somewhere warmer. "I wanted to do more busking, I like busking, and I'd outgrown the centre of Penrith. The idea grew, that I could cycle to Rome and busk along the way." So – to cut a very long story short – he loaded his bike with small panniers on the front, with the very minimum of clothes, below a lopsided bag with some poetry books and CDs. The cello, in its pink chequered case plastered with reflective yellow strips, was on an aluminium rack stretching out behind and making the bike twice as long as it would otherwise be. And then he set off, pedalling over the hills into the Yorkshire Dales, aiming for Rome.

Why, you may well ask. "It just seemed like a good idea. One of those ideas that won't go away, and the more you talk about it with other people, the more it seemed to make sense." The word pilgrimage is circumnavigated: "Though I used to be a vicar, I'm not religious anymore, but I'm very conscious of the sacredness of places. I'm always reflecting on what I'm doing, so I did learn something from the journey each day." The journey to Rome ended when he played his cello in front of St Peter's Basilica with the written permission of the Vatican City police. "I had to ask, nicely. If I'd just started playing I would have ended up in an Italian jail before you could say arrivederci."

Kenneth, I asked him, how would you like to climb a
mountain and play some music to promote your book? Yes, of
course, was the reply, and so it was that very early on a June
morning, as the heat was likely to get intense later in the day,
we set off for the short climb up Loughrigg from behind High
Close, Kenneth's cello strapped to his back. At the top, beside
the rebuilt trig column, he played *The Swan* by Saint-Saëns,
and followed it with a Gavotte by Popper, to the delight and
bemusement of early morning runners and walkers. He'd
planned to add a dance tune "which may, or may not, have
been written by Henry VIII", but we were driven away by
midges. But though he was happy to climb a mountain to play
music, he now does very little cycling. "The journey took such
a toll on my hands. And if my hands are damaged, I can't play
the cello. That's more important to me than cycling."

If that sounds bizarre, Eleanor Knowles, Ambleside
runner, teacher and musician, played the euphonium on top
of Loughrigg. She spent a very memorable night on the fell
as part of an unusual annual charity event. Light the Lakes
is a spectacular fundraiser for the charity Care of Police
Survivors (COPS) which supports families of police officers
who have sacrificed their lives in serving their communities.
At midsummer, individuals and groups climb all the
214 Wainwright peaks and light flares in their memory – at 3 in
the morning.

But at Loughrigg there's an extra dimension. A group of
brass band players from all over the UK gather in Rydal Cave
at dusk and play there. Then some of them will climb the hill

to play there as well, to coincide with the lighting of the flares across the Lake District. When Eleanor and her son Rory took part, the group included musicians from eight different brass bands, including the City of Birmingham Band, and police officers from Cambridgeshire Constabulary.

Also taking part were members of the Speakman family on their ascent to honour the memories of father and son officers, Don and Jonny Speakman. Jonny lost his life rescuing children from a dangerous rip tide, and Don walked Light the Lakes every year until he died at the age of 72.

Eleanor said: "It was a very touching experience, in memory of police officers fallen while on duty, and many of the organisers had a personal connection with the cause." She played the euphonium, and Rory was on cornet. "Some of Rory's friends walked up to the top to support us. It was a long night. We slept on the summit in the rain waiting for the time to play which coincided with the lighting of a lantern on each Wainwright summit." There were 50 musicians playing in the cave, of whom 20 went up to play on the top.

What did they play? *The Last Post* and the *National Anthem*, predictably. Less so, the Queen number *Crazy Little Thing Called Love,* requested by the family of a police officer killed on duty. And in Rydal cave, says Eleanor, "We played some beautiful hymns including *Ashoken Farewell,* and a fabulous piece called *Highland Cathedral*." Which, it happens, is my favourite bagpipe tune.

Among those upset by the damage done to the trig column on Loughrigg was Christopher Wordsworth Andrew from nearby Rydal Mount. His great great great great grandfather, the poet William Wordsworth, regularly hiked over Loughrigg – in the days before triangulation of course – with his sister Dorothy. "If you read the Journals, you can see that they would think nothing of walking ten or twenty miles in a day," says Christopher. "They had clothes that we would think totally absurd, and they had no paths to follow as we do now. In fact it's possible that William and Dorothy were the first walkers to climb up to the summit. They could certainly outwalk us if they had the gear that we have now."

Dorothy's Journals regularly mention Loughrigg, in passing; it was a part of their daily lives:

> Warm and mild, after a fine night of rain…. The woods extremely beautiful with all autumnal variety and softness. I carried a basket for mosses, and gathered some wild plants. Oh! that we had a book of botany. All flowers now are gay and deliciously sweet. The primrose still prominent; the later flowers and the shiny foxgloves very tall, with their heads budding. I went forward round the lake at the foot of Loughrigg Fell. I was much amused with the busyness of a pair of stone-chats; their restless voices as they skimmed along the water, following each other, their shadows under them, and their returning back to the stones on the shore, chirping with the same unwearied voice.
>
> *(Dorothy Wordsworth's Journal, Written at Grasmere, 14th May to 21st December 1800)*

So with the trig column restored, Christopher paid his own tribute. With young friends Ava Dove, and Billy Kennedy, who had spent the last few years studying English and reading the Romantic poets, and Moki the collie, he set off one summer morning with a book of poems in his rucksack. And Border Television camerawoman Fiona Marley Patterson also in attendance, for she'd heard that something exceptional was about to happen. At the summit, Christopher read *The World Is Too Much With Us,* to the delight of that evening's TV news viewers.

> The world is too much with us; late and soon,
> Getting and spending, we lay waste our powers;
> Little we see in Nature that is ours;
> We have given our hearts away, a sordid boon!
> This Sea that bares her bosom to the moon;
> The winds that will be howling at all hours,
> And are up-gathered now like sleeping flowers;
> For this, for everything, we are out of tune;
> It moves us not. Great God! I'd rather be
> A Pagan suckled in a creed outworn;
>
> So might I, standing on this pleasant lea,
> Have glimpses that would make me less forlorn;
> Have sight of Proteus rising from the sea;
> Or hear old Triton blow his wreathèd horn.

"It's one of the best sonnets Wordsworth wrote, perhaps the loveliest ever written," says Christopher. "Wordsworth was talking about the importance of nature over material things, money, possessions. And what a place to come and read his words, with *this* all around us.

"Loughrigg was very important to the Wordsworth family. It's right above Rydal where they lived, they could see this hill every day, and from the top here they could see all the places that they loved. William was inspired by all this. It was the centre of his life."

And from the Romantic poets to the height of romance. Dave Peacock, who's originally from Kendal, proposed to his Danish girlfriend Anna on the summit of Loughrigg. Says Dave: "The reason why I chose Loughrigg was because we started doing the Wainwrights together and I wanted somewhere with a good view, and the forecast was for low cloud." She said yes.

Soundtrack: Highland Cathedral, The Lone Piper

CHAPTER EIGHT

A LANDSCAPE FOR ARTISTS

Julian Cooper is Britain's foremost living mountain painter. He's painted and climbed in the Alps, the Himalayas and the Andes, but he retains a deep affection for lowly Loughrigg.

The fell features in a number of his early works, including some delightful scenes from the balcony of his Ambleside home where he and his artist wife Linda Ryle lived for 26 years. It was the dominant view from their window, and it is Linda who was the model for the woman in *Reading The White Goddess*, a glorious painting of Windermere from Todd Crag.

In his *Paris, Texas* painting, which features the Todd Crag end of Loughrigg, the model was Ceri Pilling, the daughter of the poet Christopher Pilling, who was living in Ambleside at the time, and was the model for many of his paintings.

And Loughrigg was, says Julian, his safety valve as life in the heart of the Lakes became ever more crowded and noisy with the growth of tourism. "It was the place to go to get away from the noise and the crush. To get away from people. It's like being in a different state of mind. You can feel your blood pressure lowering. I always came back down in a different mindset, a mental re-set. Loughrigg gives the sense of a wider reality.

"I would either head through the woods up to Todd Crag, or carry on past the golf course, and I was out, free, above it all." It gave him a great deal of inspiration, taking his sketchbook and drawing little outcrops. "And I got obsessed with the view of the Fairfield Horseshoe from various places on Loughrigg, when the light would change, especially in the evening." In one painting he has the view of Loughrigg from that direction, from Nab Scar on the northern spur of the Horseshoe. His artist acquaintance Ian Walton used to find spent bullets from one of the Loughrigg rifle ranges and used them in his work.

Julian and Linda's flat, the top two floors with a double height studio, was on the corner of Lake Road and Kelsick Road. They moved there after living in Rydal for two years; before that they had been in London. "The studio was amazing. But eventually I outgrew that and had to rent some space in a former factory in Kendal." Julian's paintings are often on a monumental scale.

Linda also painted Loughrigg scenes during that time, notably a miniature quarry which now features on her website. She recalls: "At one time I used to go up the fell every week for the exercise. I did have a slightly alarming experience on one occasion. I had veered off the path, no-one was about apart from the odd sheep, when suddenly and silently a man appeared on top of a small outcrop. He was dressed in camouflage – what we referred to then as 'survivalist' gear – and he just stood there looking across at me quietly clinking his bunch of keys. I made off pretty sharpish."

Julian says of Loughrigg: "It has two distinctive ends, very different from each other. I love the south end, looking down towards Windermere. I used to think that the northern view, beyond Grasmere over Dunmail Raise, was bleak, hostile... until I moved north." He's lived for many years in Cockermouth, his work concentrating on the fell and rock landscapes of the north-western fells.

But Julian grew up at that northern end of Loughrigg, in Grasmere, at Winterseeds. He was born there in 1947, the son of William Heaton Cooper (1903-1995) who remains one of the best-loved painters of the Lake District, as was his grandfather, Alfred Heaton Cooper (1863-1929) who established the Heaton Cooper Studio, the family business now run by Julian's niece, Becky Heaton Cooper. Julian's mother was the sculptor Ophelia Gordon Bell (1915-1975). His life has inevitably intersected with the wider currents of mountaineering and mountain painting.

He studied at Lancaster School of Art and Goldsmiths' College of Art in London, and in 1969 he was awarded the Boise Travelling Scholarship which enabled him to travel around Europe; he was resident at the British School in Rome (1969-70). He returned to the Lake District in 1975 and since then he has developed an international reputation as one of the most imaginative and thought-provoking mountain painters of his generation.

Julian has spent his working life looking for places that "carry a particular charge" for him and has found them in some of the most barren and inhospitable places on the planet: Amazonia, Andes, Himalayas, Tibet, Tasmania and Carrara in central Italy. His influences at art school were mostly, he says, "post-painterly abstraction and colour field painting", later becoming interested in the abstract expressionists.

During the 1980s and 1990s his work ranged from narrative paintings based on Malcolm Lowry's novel *Under the Volcano*, to paintings based on Wim Wenders' film *Paris, Texas*, and a series of paintings about the events surrounding the assassination of the union leader and environmentalist Chico Mendes in Amazonia in 1989.

He then went on to find new subjects among mountains, working in the Alps, the Cordillera Blanca in the Peruvian Andes, Kanchenjunga in Nepal, and Mount Kailas in Tibet. More recently he has concentrated on studying the landscape within a twenty mile radius of his home in the northern fells of the Lake District, becoming increasingly fascinated with the interplay of nature and culture, the working landscape past and present. He exhibits regularly in London, and in recent years he's had a number of exhibitions on home territory at the Heaton Cooper Studio's archive gallery.

One of these was *Among Mountains,* an exhibition of 'hardcore' paintings of some of the world's greatest mountain ranges, and covering 25 years of his life and work. They were all the result of his own adventures as a painter of mountain landscapes, fraught with danger and risk. On one occasion, working from a base camp on the Andean watershed, he carried 40 tubes of paint, a 7x6ft canvas and its alloy frame another 1000ft higher to his working site on a moraine edge. For five days he fought against the altitude to make a painting while seracs cracked off, stones fell, glacial dust was blown up from the cliff below, and cracks started appearing in the ground behind and in front of him. "Slicing off like salami, the earth eroded right up to my canvas," he recalls. He decided it was too dangerous to stay.

Another recent exhibition, *Inherited Landscapes,* was truly a family affair, featuring the work of Alfred, William, and Julian who chose four paintings by each artist and was filmed making the selections for a Channel 4 TV documentary.

"This family has been around for three generations dealing with the same landscape," he says. "But our way of looking at it has changed over time, and with different temperaments and differing attitudes to painting which influence how we see the natural world." For many years the paintings and books by Alfred and William have influenced the way the landscape of the Lake District has been viewed, and the studio is recognised as one of Cumbria's most distinguished galleries and the pre-eminent centre for landscape art in the Lake District.

We were talking in the cafe at the Heaton Cooper studio, named after Julian's grandmother, Mathilde Valentinsen, the young country girl from Norway who fell in

love with an English painter, and together they founded this
dynasty of great landscape artists. The family is all around us.
On the main wall, taking up the entire height of the room,
is one of Julian's truly monumental paintings, Scafell Crag,
a giant at 13 feet high and 10 feet wide, which has a story
almost as remarkable as the painting itself. It was commis-
sioned by the Mountain Heritage Trust at the Rheged centre
near Penrith, to celebrate mountaineering and the role of the
Lake District in the birth of rock climbing.

Julian began working on it in his studio 25 years ago,
but when the site for the painting was changed, moving to a
new space that was higher than wider, it had to be re-scaled.
"Pikes Crag had to be moved in front of Scafell, deleting the
landscape in between," says Julian.

Then the opening date of Rheged was brought forward,
because the then Prime Minister, Tony Blair, would be
available to carry out the official opening, and so Julian's
painting had to be hung unfinished. Hanging the painting
took four men, ropes, two long ladders, and a specially made
framework to support it while it was secured to the wall.

And then after the ceremony was over, the painting
was removed to a barn where Julian added climbers on the
crag, friends whom he persuaded to model for him. Among
them was his niece Becky, whose outstretched hand can be
seen in the painting. The finished work was then taken back
to Rheged six months later, where it hung for 20 years, before
moving to Grasmere and its new home.

Here, from the cafe window, the dominant fell in the

scene is Stone Arthur with its craggy bastions. Step outside and look round to the north and there's the famous outline of Helm Crag, the 'lion and the lamb' summit. These and so many more feature in the work of all the Heaton Cooper artists, but it's to Loughrigg that each returned, time and again.

In *The Hills of Lakeland*, published in 1938, William Heaton Cooper wrote: "It (Loughrigg) is typical of many of the low hills that children adopt as their favourite playground. On it are innumerable hills and valleys and shallow tarns which appear and disappear and freeze earlier than the big sheets of water. The formation is so complicated that even Tom Chapman, who used to farm Brow Head on its slopes, said that he had been 'fair boddered to find t'road yam (the road home) when it's a li'le bit misty-like'.

"For many years my father (that's Alfred Heaton Cooper) had a small hut just below the summit where we would go and camp for days on end, living like savages, cooking on a trench oven, swimming in the tarns and falling off rocks – the very best holiday education for youngsters. We would sleep out on the dry turf in the heat of summer and wake up with the dew on our faces. One morning, as I lay half-awake gazing into the eyes of the sun that shone whitely through the morning mist, two elegant figures, which might have been of almost any size, danced across the grass against the light. They seemed to embrace and fall away again till they came to a round hillock. Round and round it, then up to the top in another embrace, they went. As I rubbed my eyes to make certain it was not a dream, the two fighting weasels saw me and disappeared into a jungle of bracken."

Jane Renouf, writer and historian, was told that Alfred asked his artist friends to leave an original drawing or painting on the walls of the hut, but vandals broke in and the paintings were all destroyed. Jane interviewed William when she was writing a biography of Alfred (*Alfred Heaton Cooper, Painter of Landscape*, Red Bank Press, 1997.) AHC, she writes, was among the first of many Victorian painters to illustrate the natural beauty of the Lake District landscape. Born in 1864, he grew up in Bolton where his parents were mill workers. "They made many sacrifices to provide a good education for their children and it soon became clear that Alfred had a talent for art."

He won a scholarship to Westminster School of Art, his student days coinciding with the emergence of Impressionism out of the new realism explored by artists such as Constable. But Alfred developed a style of his own, and abandoned formal education to try and make a living by his art. He met Mathilde when his love of the natural world took him to the Norwegian fjords, then a popular resort for wealthy Victorian tourists, and they came back together to the Lakes. He had a prolific painting career, and many reproductions of his work are sold every year. He also illustrated tourist guidebooks to Britain and Europe, and though he had little financial reward in his own lifetime, he was the inspiration and foundation for the unique family painting tradition.

William Heaton Cooper told Jane (Ambleside Oral

History Archive interview) about his father's role in the local defence corps in World War 1. "He had a rifle, it was very exciting. They built a hut, a wee hut, which after the War and after the local volunteers had finished, my father rented for ten shillings a year just to have for us children. A marvellous time we had. We had lots of friends coming and staying there with us, mostly it was just during the school holidays, we just ran wild up there. We took food up and cooked it ourselves. Those were very happy days, and I thought it was very nice of my father to do that. And he had become very fond of Loughrigg. He could climb as far as that, there was no rock climbing involved. Well, all these fells you could get up to the top without any rock climbing. But Loughrigg he painted from. You can see, as you go to different points of Loughrigg, you can see new views of Langdale and so on, and little tarns, spots of water too. I think those were the happiest painting places."

Becky Heaton Cooper has very distinct memories of her grandfather, William. "Anyone would think that open water or 'wild' swimming was an invention of the 21st century. Yes, it is enjoying immense popularity at the moment, but I'm very proud to reflect that my grandfather, who died in 1995, was a pioneer as a swimmer as well as an artist."

William was a remarkable man, says Becky, an outdoor painter who did much of his work on the spot – often high up in the fells – and then completing it in his studio. He was a rock climber, taking part in several first ascents on Lakeland crags and having links with the pioneers of the

sport, and his expert knowledge of the crags is evident in his
mountain paintings. His meticulous drawings of the crags,
the routes carefully delineated, have long been used in the
official climbing guides to the crags, which he illustrated for
decades, and he was an honorary member of the Fell and Rock
Climbing Club. But in the hollows of his beloved fells and
rocks, in the many tarns of the Lake District, he would swim,
and he would paint those beautiful waters. Of the three major
books of his paintings, *The Tarns of Lakeland* (1960) has been
hailed as a masterpiece, for the quality of his sensitive writing
as well as his exquisite art.

"William was in his seventies when I was young, so
he didn't join us on many family outings, but his spirit of
adventure lived on in my father, John, and my uncle Julian,
and was deeply ingrained in us all. Family days out with dad
and my two brothers usually involved us all piling into a very
old Land Rover and heading off to explore the nearby caves,
quarries and lakes.

"Later, I was driven to seek out many places that were
dear to my grandfather. We spent many summers swimming
at Penny Rock on Grasmere with dad and the family, jumping
off rocks and playing in the weir. Grandfather painted one
of my favourite paintings there, unusually for a landscape
artist, one that depicts his family: my grandmother, my father
and uncle Julian are there. I still have lovely memories of dad
lighting campfires there as the light faded towards the end of
the day. We all knew the faint, tree-lined path well enough in
the dark, it took us back to the tiny hole in the wall where the

Land Rover waited. I still know that path well to this day and it still evokes childhood thoughts of pixies and fairies.

"Living now on the shores of Loughrigg Tarn, my own children have taken to the water with that same spirit of adventure. And while a great deal is written now about places to swim, here and in other wild places, grandfather's book remains the very best guide to swimming in the Lake District. His knowledge of the local geography, geology and history add so much of value, along with the obvious passion for this beautiful landscape."

And there's another connection which takes us back to Julian Cooper. In 1979 he was asked to design the cover for a small book of poems by Fleur Adcock, the New Zealand-born poet who, for a year, had been writer in residence at Ambleside's Charlotte Mason College, now part of the University of Cumbria. This collection is *Beyond Loughrigg*, published by Bloodaxe. According to her publisher, Fleur Adcock was "romantically addicted to English trees and flowers" as a child. She settled in London, but returning to the countryside to live below Loughrigg Fell in the Lake District, she rediscovered this love for nature.

"Despite qualms about recording 'what is famous', she responded to the Lakes with freshness and vitality. Her exhilaration is clearly expressed in this selection of poems from 'a year among lakes and fells'. However, as a writer in residence at a college, her stay in Cumbria was short-lived; afterwards, she returned to her old job in London. This is the burden of *Below Loughrigg*: that writer of these forceful poems is now back in the city." (Fleur Adcock, *Collected Poems* Bloodaxe Books, 2024).

Fleur Adcock CNZM OBE was born in 1934 in New Zealand of English and Northern Irish ancestry, though she has lived much of her life in England. She is well-represented in New Zealand poetry anthologies, was awarded an honorary doctorate of literature from Victoria University of Wellington, and was awarded an OBE in 1996 for her contribution to New Zealand literature. In 2008 she was made a Companion of the New Zealand Order of Merit, for services to literature. This tiny, early collection of poems resonates with all who know and love Loughrigg Fell, even to the practicalities of a walk:

How far is it around this sprawling fell?
I've come perhaps three miles. Will it be four,
Or less, the Grasmere way? It's hard to tell.

She writes of the hounds in the kennels above Nook Lane (which I heard howling every morning for the 13 years I lived on the estate just below there), she writes of rainbows, three in one morning, and the flooded rivers Rothay and Brathay, of ravens and snow on the tops and fungi, and Wordsworth would be pleased. There's more about Fleur Adcock in Chapter 9.

Artist Liz Wakelin sketches these fine details of life in and around Loughrigg. Her first book, *Sketching a Year in Lakeland* (Inspired by Lakeland) captures 52 weeks of the year 2022, in hand-written notes (in the manner of Wainwright) and exquisite water-colours. The whole of Lakeland is here, but Liz lives in Ambleside and spend a lot of her time walking and running – and sketching – on Loughrigg, so it's obvious that this corner of the South Lakes would be well represented. Liz first came to the Lakes in 1976. "At first Loughrigg wasn't on my radar because I was obsessed with the high fells. I don't know when I first went up there. But I love it now."

The book is a personal journal that Liz, mountaineer, cyclist, runner, adventurer and immensely talented artist, is very happy to share. It's the tale of her life during those 12 months, her walks around the fells, the cycle rides with husband Barry, visits to the local bookshop and ironmonger and, above all, tea and cakes in many pictorially-perfect cafes. The result is a treasury of colour and memory which says more, perhaps, about the nature and character of the Lake District than any other single volume. Dorothy Wordsworth had pioneered the notion of a Journal from her home at Rydal, and this is a tradition into which Liz has tapped, even running a course in journal sketching at William Wordsworth's former home at Rydal Mount.

Readers have fallen in love with the delicacy of her colours, the detail of leaf and petal, the humour on faces of people walking and sitting and chatting. There are images of high mountains, of course, including a spectacular panorama of Fairfield and the Helvellyn range from Place Fell. But among the sketches are jars of marmalade and honey on a stall at Keswick market, teapots and tea-cosies, stiles and gate-latches, sheep and lambs, and above all flowers. Wood anemone, primrose, celandine and of course oceans of daffodils.

As a young woman Liz climbed all over the UK and in the Alps, ticking off ascents such as the Mont Blanc de Tacul, and the south west face of the Aiguille du Midi. She's also a more than competent runner, though she maintains that she just runs to keep fit for other activities. That said, she's run the London Marathon, twice took first place in the 36-mile Calderdale Hike, and recently took part in the gruelling Montane Lakeland 50 ultra race. Until recently she was also a Duke of Edinburgh gold award assessor, and she and Barry have been cycle touring throughout the UK and in France and Greece.

At school she was told she was no good at art, and should study French instead. "If I'm told I can't do something, it's like a red rag to a bull. When I wasn't allowed to study art, I started to teach myself, at first just copying others' work. It took a long time before I could be original. I needed to believe in myself, and learn to like what I was doing." Her French, she adds, is poor.

She's always kept a journal, and increasingly made sketches while out walking, or took photos from which she could later create sketches. And it was during lockdown, with time on her hands, that she would share some of her work on social media, finding a kindred spirit in West Cumbrian artist and writer Alan Cleaver. And it was he who drew the attention of Liz's work to his friend, the publisher Dave Felton, of Inspired by Lakeland.

But it was Loughrigg we both wanted to talk about one afternoon at Rydal Mount. What's special about this little fell? A great deal, says Liz. "I love the way that it sprawls. I do like pointy mountains, but there's so much of Loughrigg, you can lose yourself on it even if you know it really well. There are gremlins there that move the paths, and if the mist comes down I always end up in Black Mire. And because it sprawls, there's lots of little nooks and crannies, it's never the same from one day to the next."

And for an artist, there are so many different viewpoints, and so many different colours. "The gold, the bronze, the browns in autumn are magnificent. The cairns, the pikes, the peaks, are never the same." She takes a lot of photos on the hills, but if she's going onto Loughrigg to make a sketch, it's done in situ, with her notebook and pencil. "There's something about sitting and drawing that makes you look so deeply at something that everything else is lost. You focus on that one scene, that one object for so long that by the time you've finished drawing it, you really *know* it properly. It's much more intimate than taking a photograph. You haven't stood and stared to take a photo, and that's why, when you draw, you are totally immersed, and all hell could break loose around you. It's like reading a good book when you're unaware of what's going on around you. Sometimes I've looked up and there's a crowd of people watching me, and I'd not realised. I'm unaware of them because my focus is on whatever it is that I'm drawing.

"There's so much. There's something about low fells; at first I used to head for the big mountains and into the high hills, but the variety of scenery that you got on and around a lower fell like Loughrigg, and the fact that you're looking up at the big mountains, they're much more visually appealing. If you go off the beaten track and explore a bit further there's so much to see. You can go up to Lily Tarn by the main path, but if you scramble around over the rocks, off the paths, you could spend your whole life there and still not know every inch of it.

"There are so many sketching opportunities. I do tend to get caught by the same ones. I like Lily Tarn, because if you sketch something more than once, it's like discovering another side to somebody's personality. You hone your skills, and after a while the motor skills become ingrained, so you've got the muscle memory that means you can draw it, and you can catch it quickly, and you don't miss that moment, when the sun is beating or the clouds are passing. So although there's variety on Loughrigg, I like that repetition as well.

"It's the same with paths, learning them so well that you know where every stone is." Which came in useful in the early winter of 2023 when Ambleside was besieged after a dramatically heavy snowfall. Liz and Barry decided to walk up to Lily Tarn in the dark, with headtorches, and found a transformed world but still, instinctively, knew where the path was.

"It was good snow. It wasn't dangerous snow, it wasn't icy, it was soft, and we could just about see where the paths were. It was really hard work, and it was difficult to get photographs because our headtorches wouldn't shine far enough. We didn't see a soul. But we know the area so well, that route. It was magical."

She loves every season on the hill as an artist, except summer. "I don't like summer. I think it's because the colours are just green, and green – apart from being a really difficult colour to capture in paint – is a monotone. So the variety of colour over spring, autumn and winter is what I find really engaging. The green of summer leaves me cold. And I don't like bracken. I like it when it's dead for its fantastic colour. And Loughrigg is smothered in it."

She likes to know that where the bluebells are today in spring would once have been wooded. "Wouldn't it be amazing if there were still patches of woodland up there? There is planting going on, and there are fewer sheep grazing now, so we might get a resurgence of deciduous woodland."

Her face lights up at the mention of bluebells, though she says they are "phenomenally difficult" to draw and capture in colour. "The colour is a bit like Loughrigg itself, it just escapes you. It's not blue and it's not really purple. And of course sometimes it's pink and there are white ones as well. And the shape; sometimes you end up with something so stylised it looks twee, if you're not careful. Though the bluebells on the side of Loughrigg heading down to Grasmere do make an amazing carpet."

Other flowers on Loughrigg she loves include the bogbean in Lily Tarn, "the complexity of the flowers, and when you get up close, it's a fascinating plant. The other one is bog asphodel, the yellow, it's an orangey yellow, like tiny orchids, up close it's not one flower, it's a head of flowers. You can see great swathes of this orange-yellow across all the boggy bits, and as they die they become a really lovely russet. With the seasons the colour flows across the landscape."

Liz notes that there are not many trees on Loughrigg that stand out. "There's a dying ash tree beyond the second gate at Pine Rigg, and there's a copse of larch trees that's now been felled. But wildlife! Seared into my memory is seeing a sparrowhawk take a small creature and fly away with it, maybe a vole or mouse, and it was just one of those special moments."

Loughrigg, she says, was her parents last fell, at the age of 80, before they stopped climbing the hills. "There's a picture of us all sitting on the summit, all the family."

And we move on, in the next chapter, from artists to writers, to which my lovely friend Penny Bradshaw was going to contribute, but ended up writing so much that the chapter is hers alone.

Soundtrack: Peer Gynt Suite No 1, In the hall of the mountain king, Edvard Grieg

CHAPTER NINE

LITERARY LOUGHRIGG

By Penny Bradshaw

In his *Literary Associations of the English Lakes* (1894), Canon Hardwicke Rawnsley, co-founder of the National Trust, writes of the literary ghosts who inhabit the English Lake District, and it might be argued that the unassuming Loughrigg Fell and its immediate environs are home to more than a fair share of such 'ghostly presences'.

Dorothy and William Wordsworth regularly passed over or skirted the base of this fell in their journeyings from Grasmere or Rydal to the nearest market town of Ambleside. In one of the earliest entries in her *Grasmere Journals*, Dorothy writes: 'The prospect exceeding beautiful from Loughrigg fell. It was so green, that no eye could be weary of reposing upon it' (May 1800). Then at the start of June she records lying on the ground 'upon the steep of Loughrigg' with 'my heart dissolved in what I saw'.

In August of that same year, the Wordsworths' great friend and fellow poet, Samuel Taylor Coleridge, visited Dove Cottage and Dorothy describes how she, her brother, and

Coleridge 'walked a long time upon Loughrigg & returned in the grey twilight' with the moon 'just setting as we reached home'.

The views from Loughrigg were ones of which the Wordsworth siblings never tired, and many years later William Wordsworth celebrated the sight of Grasmere viewed from Loughrigg Terrace in his poem, *The Excursion* (1814):

> We clomb a green hill's side; and as we clomb,
> The Valley, opening out her bosom, gave
> Fair prospect, intercepted less and less,
> O'er the flat meadows and indented coast
> Of the smooth lake, in compass seen: – far off,
> And yet conspicuous, stood the old Church-tower,
> In majesty presiding over fields
> And habitations seemingly preserved
> From all intrusion of the restless world
> By rocks impassable and mountains huge.

Though the Wordsworths loved to walk on Loughrigg, enjoying the views it offered of the 'unity' and seclusion of the vale of Grasmere, at other times they would sit on the opposite side of the valley and look out towards Loughrigg itself. In March 1802, Dorothy records that she climbed White Moss and looked across to see Loughrigg illuminated by moonlight:

> … as I climbed Moss the moon came out from behind
> a Mountain Mass of Black Clouds – O the unutterable
> darkness of the sky & the Earth below the Moon! & the
> glorious brightness of the moon itself! There was a vivid

sparkling streak of light at this end of Rydale water but the
rest was very dark & Loughrigg fell & Silver How were white
& bright as if they were covered with hoar frost.

In a journal entry from May of that same year, Dorothy notes
the way that Loughrigg catches the very last light of the sun as
it sets:

Oh the overwhelming beauty of the vale below – greener than
green. Two Ravens flew high high in the sky & the sun shone
upon their bellys & their wings long after there was none of
his light to be seen but a little space on the top of Loughrigg
Fell.

The spectacle of the sun setting on Loughrigg was also picked
up by William Wordsworth in a sonnet he wrote during
the Rydal Mount years (1813–1850). The 'rocky parapet'
mentioned in the poem is the summit of Loughrigg Fell and
he told his friend Isabella Fenwick that 'Not once only, but a
hundred times, have the feelings of the sonnet been awakened
by the same objects seen from the same place':

Now the horizon's rocky parapet
Is reached, where, forfeiting his bright attire,
He burns--transmuted to a dusky fire--
Then pays submissively the appointed debt
To the flying moments, and is seen no more.

It was not though only the summit and heights of Loughrigg
which were important to the Wordsworths in their physical
and imaginative engagement with place. They also spent

plenty of time on ground level, walking the lane which winds along the foot of Loughrigg on its eastern side, alongside the River Rothay. The lane which accompanies the Rothay as it passes the base of Loughrigg Fell is known as 'Under Loughrigg' (though it is often referred to by Dorothy as 'Clappersgate'), and it is described by William Wordsworth in his *Guide to the Lakes* as one of the most 'interesting' walks which can be taken from Ambleside. It was indeed a route which he and Dorothy took regularly on their outings and is referenced on numerous occasions in Dorothy's journals.

In the years following the arrival of the Wordsworths in Grasmere, this short lane 'under Loughrigg fell' would go on to become home to a number of writers with Wordsworthian connections. Thomas De Quincey, author of *Confessions of an English Opium-Eater*, who had rented Dove Cottage after the Wordsworths had left, lived at a house on this lane called Fox Ghyll between 1820–1825. The house was later described by the novelist, journalist and social reformer, Harriet Martineau, who moved to Ambleside in the 1840s, as 'sheltered and almost overhung by the perpendicular wooded side of Loughrigg'. It is now the home of Paul Mann, the Lord of the Manor of Loughrigg.

Another literary family who took up residence along 'Under Loughrigg' were the Arnolds. Dr Thomas Arnold, headmaster of Rugby School, had a holiday house called Fox How built here in 1833 at the suggestion of Wordsworth. After this, Arnold's family, including his son Matthew and his granddaughter, Mary, would visit regularly and both would themselves go on to become significant literary figures in the Victorian period – Matthew Arnold as a poet and Mary as a novelist who published under her married name, Mrs Humphrey Ward.

Briefly, William Wordsworth's beloved daughter, Dora would also settle at another house along this lane following her marriage to Edward Quillinan. The house was called Loughrigg Holme, but it would be their marital home for a very short time, since tragically Dora would die of tuberculosis in 1847 at the age of 43, within a year of moving into the house.

Edward Quillinan continued to receive literary visitors at Loughrigg Holme until his own death in 1851 and it was here that Matthew Arnold first met both Harriet Martineau and Charlotte Brontë, a meeting which is memorialised in Arnold's poem, 'Haworth Churchyard', written following Brontë's death in 1855. The poem opens with these lines:

Where, under Loughrigg, the stream
Of Rotha sparkles through fields
Vested for ever with green,
Four years since, in the house
Of a gentle spirit, now dead –
Wordsworth's son-in-law, friend –
I saw the meeting of two
Gifted women.

The beauty of this lane and its surrounding fields, sheltered as they are by the slopes of Loughrigg and 'Vested for ever with green', also comes through vividly in Harriet Martineau's *A Year at Ambleside*. Martineau records walking 'along the foot of Loughrigg' in March 1846 to gather plants for the garden of her newly built house in Ambleside, The Knoll, and she leaves us with a picture of a lane winding through a landscape which is abundant with spring flowers and natural beauty:

> The fences are tufted with wall-plants, which look tempting... . [B]efore entering the birch copse of Fox How, we must help ourselves to primroses from the new clearing where they so abound as to give a yellow hue to the hillside, as seen from our windows. The blossoms nestle under every clump of suckers, and at the base of every sprout of rock. While we have our trowels in use, we take up wood anemones and sorrel with a view to variegating the carpet of the copse... The next abode is Mr Q's, where we must beg our daffodils.

Martineau was also already well aware of the area's pre-existing literary connections and this is something with which later literary visitors have continued to engage and, at times, with which they have wrestled.

During the winter of 1977–78 the New Zealand-born poet, Fleur Adcock, took up the role of writer-in-residence at the Charlotte Mason College, now the University of Cumbria's Ambleside campus. She published a small volume of poems, *Below Loughrigg* (1979), which were inspired by this residency. Within the opening poem in the collection, Adcock describes how she finds this place both 'Inspiring and inhibiting' and, in subsequent poems, writes of walking the landscapes which had so shaped Wordsworth's poetry. In the poem 'Mid-Point' Adcock finds herself walking on and round Loughrigg, 'this sprawling fell', and wondering whether or not to turn back. Seeing the 'tarn, spangled with quick refractions / Of sunlight', she is inspired to go on, adding: 'I'll take heart/from gazing down again on Rydal Water./The point of no return was at the start'.

It's a poem in which, after an experience of personal struggle, Adcock seems to begin to find her own inspiration in this place. In another poem in the collection ('The Vale of Grasmere'), she makes more explicit both her encounters with the area's ghostly literary presences and the possibility of carving out her own voice through personal experiences of walking these fells:

> Most of the rocks are wreathed by now
> with faded rags of fluttering soul.
> But the body finds another function
> for crags and fells, as Wordsworth knew
> himself: they offer hands and feet
> their own creative work to do.

Rawnsley's ghosts are still in evidence in *Below Loughrigg*, but the poems also offer a sense of this as an evolving literary landscape, since Adcock finds here, what she describes in one poem as, a 'clear channel flowing' ('Writer in Residence') and this suggests that she has been able to develop her own imaginative engagement with this 'sprawling fell' and its environs.

Dr Penny Bradshaw is an Associate Professor of English Literature at the University of Cumbria and author of *A Literary Walking Tour of Ambleside* (Inspired by Lakeland, 2021).

Soundtrack: The Lark Ascending, Vaughan Williams

CHAPTER TEN

OUR MOUNTAIN

W e all love the owl that nests near the foot of Loughrigg, but Julie Coldwell knows a man who has befriended a raven on the hill. It's a delightful and rather moving story, and Julie will tell it herself later in a very beautiful tribute to her favourite mountain. David Cooper saw Loughrigg lit up with glow-worms and he, too, will tell that story himself.

Loughrigg is a special place for many people. One New Years Day, a few years ago, Judith Keely lost a grey pearl earring on the fell – and found it again, almost by magic. The earring had sentimental value, a gift from Australia from her late husband, and Judith, a retired teacher living in Ambleside who walks over Loughrigg regularly, heard it fall as it hit her boot while she was adjusting her hat not far from the summit. "It disappeared. Nowhere to be found. Is it any wonder, falling on a grey slate and shingle path." The friends walking with her searched the ground. One of them built a tiny cairn to mark the spot where it had fallen, so they could continue the search on their way back down.

At the summit they tested a bivouac shelter which was a Christmas present for one of the party, Jo. They all squeezed in, including Marion with her arm in plaster, and Poppy the dog, they ate their sandwiches, then headed back down. And on the descent, beside the hurriedly built cairn, there it was. "Jo spotted it at once. She caught a glimpse of something glinting on the path, and there it was, one grey pearl earring. I could hardly believe it. We had somehow returned down the identical route we'd gone up, something I almost never do. What a lucky, happy lady I was!"

Many people have special memories of Loughrigg. Eleanor Knowles who, you might remember, played the euphonium on the summit, recalls that in her family in the 1970s and early 1980s "we would always break in anyone's new walking boots on Loughrigg. It was a tradition. We were always very well kitted out."

And another family story. On a prominent outcrop below Todd Crag on the south side of Loughrigg is a memorial bench. It's the third bench up on the path from Clappersgate, a path that leads to a well-loved viewpoint. The bench has a memorial plaque, named for Dennis Shipman, an enthusiastic walker who loved the Lakes and visited regularly with the Ansty Hill Walkers club from Coventry. He died in 1997, and his family chose this location for the bench in his memory.

His grandson, Stephen, a head teacher from Hinckley in Leicestershire, also loves the Lakes, and wanted to encourage his children to walk up to the bench when they were on holiday, and even left a tin of Brasso up there so that the plaque could be polished. And as an enticement to son Tait and daughter Esme, he and his wife Kerry started a game in the spirit of geo-caching. Along with the brass polish, he left a small visitors' book with a request that other walkers might sign it, add their comments, and perhaps email a photo to them. "It was initially a ruse to get my son to walk to the top," says Stephen. But it became a family tradition with a wider impact. For ten years, books have been left, signed, and returned to the Shipman family who love to read the comments, sometimes a little damp, or even nibbled at the edges. The brass polish has been used, too.

"We try to visit a couple of times a year, usually on a Thursday so we can have coffee in the Holy Trinity church hall at Brathay before starting the climb," Stephen said. "Most of the books make it back to us, as we leave a request for each to be returned when it's full. Visitors write comments, and send us photos. It is always nice to get an email with a photo of a shiny plaque and the magnificent view. We keep all the books and when the grandchildren meet up we all have a read and remember."

This deserved an expedition of its own after learning about the Shipman family in late summer 2023. It was a misty Sunday morning, with heavy traffic on the road below at Clappersgate but not a soul on the path as I started to climb up through Fishgarths wood. This is a place we usually visit in spring for the outrageously overpowering display of bluebells. The path levels after a short and harsh climb, following a narrow trod above a steep wooded ravine, and here is the first memorial bench, dedicated to Sid and Jammy Cross. The view from here has been obscured now by significant tree growth; Sid died in 1998. He and Jammy (Alice was her Sunday best name) were legends in the mountaineering world for most of the 20th century.

Sid was a climber and pioneer of mountain rescue, most notably from his base at the Old Dungeon Ghyll Hotel at the head of Great Langdale where he ruled as mine host for more than 20 years. Born in Kendal in 1913 he discovered rock climbing at the age of 14, during a Sunday School outing to Langdale. For his first big climb, the intimidating pinnacle of Napes Needle, on Great Gable, he borrowed a length of old coffin rope and wore rubber galoshes. His successors in the mountain rescue teams today would absolutely not approve.

But Sid trained as a cobbler so that he could make his own suitable boots, and then bought a dilapidated pub in Eskdale. This was the Burnmoor Inn at Boot (now smart, and returned to its original name of the Boot Inn) which became a popular haunt of walkers and climbers. In 1949 the Crosses took over the Old Dungeon Ghyll hotel where Sid had helped out in the kitchen in his teens. This gave him a base from which to bring together the various volunteers who helped when there were incidents or accidents in the mountains, and from where he also helped set up the Search and Rescue Dog Association.

The 1950s had seen saw a huge increase in the numbers of people who took up rock-climbing as a sport. It was during this period that climbing became more accessible to ordinary people, as opposed to the leisured classes whose preserve it had previously been. With a post-war increase in affluence and increasing personal mobility, many lads, and occasionally lasses, from the northern cities began to make weekend trips to the Lakes, camping rough or in farmers' barns, especially in Langdale, and many of them later became climbing legends themselves. Unfortunately, lots of them started falling off crags and desperate and dramatic rescues became more frequent. Thus was born the Langdale Mountain Rescue team and when it amalgamated with Ambleside in 1969, Cross remained president almost until his death.

And here they are, in spirit, Sid and his wife looking across the tops of the trees down the lake, with their beloved Langdale just around the corner. A little higher, there's a second bench dedicated to the memory of Joe and Win Connell, and no one so far has been able to tell me who they were. Then the path bifurcates; ignore the yellow arrow pointing left and downhill, and instead climb quite steeply again through woodland that still bears the scars of Storm Arwen, which brought down so many trees around here in the late autumn of 2021. Through another gate, and the Shipman bench is immediately on the right. Not much of a view on this misty morning, but tucked away underneath, covered with three pieces of slate, is the plastic box containing the latest version of the notebook, and three pens... just in case! A lovely reflective way to spend a Sunday morning.

And then, down came the mist, and lost in thought I became lost in reality. After all these years, Loughrigg can still play tricks, so many tiny paths and sheep-trods, and that sinking feeling that someone's been up here and moved Lily Tarn. Again.

Heather Jones can be found at the summit of Loughrigg regularly, always in the company of a toy called Zippy. Originally from Canada, Heather has lived and worked all over the world, including New Zealand and Australia, but always comes back to this corner of the Lake District, and now she lives just across the A593 from her beloved hill.

"Ambleside feels like home," she says. And when she first came here, Loughrigg was the first fell she climbed. "I've done a lot of walking in the Lake District now, but Loughrigg is the hill I've been up the most." Not always to the summit, though, for Heather seeks out peace and solitude on her mountain, and has found nooks and crannies where she can get away from people, sit and watch the view, or read a book. "Wainwright says everyone likes Loughrigg, and he's right. It's at the centre of everything here, like a hub, with every type of terrain you can imagine.

"But that means it's very popular, and I like to avoid people when I'm out walking. Loughrigg is my place for solace, and so I seldom visit the trig point at the summit because there's usually somebody there." Though she does take with her the Beanie-baby toy, Zippy, who has travelled the world with her and has been on every walk up Loughrigg for 21 years.

Heather's also something of an artist, and has recently taken up needlefelting (fibre art). But she seldom spends very long indoors, as the lure of Loughrigg is so strong. "I never tire of it, and I never tire of the view from Todd Crag." This is the outcrop closest to where she lives and works, where she might go at the beginning or the end of a working day, to take photos, to look out for buzzards, or badgers, or just *be* there. Her favourite walk is in the spring, the ascent via Fishgarths wood when the bluebells cover the hillside.

"I look for the beauty every time, and I find it. I guess my favourite time and place is winter at Lily Tarn, when it freezes over, and the light is low. I can sit on the bench and know that I'm not likely to come across many people."

Jim Tyson lives at the foot of Ambleside's other mountain, Wansfell, but there's no question about which is his favourite. Loughrigg tops them all, even Scafell Pike and Helvellyn, in Jim's eyes. And he knows the fell better than most.

Jim, artist, cartoonist, runner and parent helper with Ambleside AC's junior squad, has been wandering over Loughrigg since childhood. He grew up in Ambleside, living on Compston Road very close to the fell access through Rothay Park. "It was just an extension to the park for us. We used to go up to Lily Tarn and play hide and seek, hiding in the bracken. Amazingly, we never got bitten by ticks."

He recalls camping on the fell as a youngster, certainly while he was still at primary school. "I was probably nine when we first camped out. I remember my dad coming up to check on us before we went to sleep, and then coming up again in the morning. And then, in our teens, we would still be camping up there but without a tent, just a sleeping bag.

Lying there looking up at the sky, it was like a paint brush had scattered stars all above us. One morning, very early, I woke to see a stag watching us, checking us out. It was magical."

The freedom to roam and explore echoes Becky Heaton Cooper's childhood memories of Loughrigg, and for Jim the fell has always been a special place. "There's so much of it, you can always get away from other people, and yet it's so accessible." He started running while at school, and won both the school fell race, and the Rushbearing race up to Todd Crag. "For the school race we had to run in our plimsolls, pumps, we called them, but for the Rushbearing race we could wear fell shoes. Mine were Walshes."

He's since taken part in many races up and down and over the hill and loves to see the next generation of runners training on his familiar turf, ostensibly playing games as all children love to do. "We had the kids doing relay races around the tarn dressed in Hallowe'en gear. There was lots of screaming, and they were having such fun. There was no stress which might have been there if you called it a formal training session."

As a teenager he would sit on Todd Crag and look down the length of Windermere and imagine that the future lay somewhere down there, in 'the south'. In fact, Jim went to study art further north, in Carlisle, and Kendal was the furthest south he ever lived – "Life isn't in the south, it's *here*" – though he enjoys city breaks for the cultural excitement. "Though when you live here, the pace in a city is so tiring after a couple of days."

Jim started swimming in Loughrigg Tarn after Long
Covid affected his ability to run. "Nothing felt right. But
I read that cold water therapy might help, and I started
swimming in the tarn. It's true, it does give you the same
endorphin rush." He's maintained the habit and still swims
there regularly with friends." He says that there's always
"something to get out of Loughrigg", even if it's just to walk to
Chester's cafe along the bridleway, or walk to Rydal cave. He
loves the view north from the summit trig point, noting that
you can see Great Calva, the furthest north of the hills visited
on the Bob Graham round. "And from Great Calva you can
see into Scotland."

Suzanne Fairless-Aitken used to bribe her children with
chocolate buttons to get them to climb higher on Loughrigg.
Now, in their teens, they race ahead, and for good measure,
run down and jump in Loughrigg Tarn afterwards. Suzanne
lives in Hexham where she works for Bloodaxe Books,
the internationally renowned publisher of literature and
poetry, but the family visit the Lakes whenever possible. Her
husband's family used to live near Carlisle.

She sees Loughrigg as a great 'starter' fell, like Catbells.
"It's so rewarding. It's not just straight up and down, you can
stay up there for a long time." Which is what they did on a
recent visit, staying with six other families at the High Close
YHA just at the foot of Loughrigg above Elterwater. "We
climbed from the door of the hostel, a group of all ranges
of ability. The teenagers just ran up, and we had a picnic on
the summit." Son Archie took some dramatic photos with

his drone camera, and the whole group swam in Grasmere afterwards.

"I love the sense of being dwarfed by nature. When you go there, no matter what's going on in your life, no matter what you're going through, it puts everything into perspective. You can be genuinely over-awed by the experience, and then go back feeling better for it. It's always worth the pilgrimage."

Kerry Darbishire is a songwriter, author and poet who lives in a farmhouse not far from the foot of Loughrigg. Her first collection *A Lift of Wings*, 2014, and her second, *Distance Sweet on my Tongue*, 2018, were both published by Indigo Dreams Publishing. *Kay's Ark*, the story of her mother, was published by Handstand Press in 2016. Her pamphlet *A Window of Passing Light* was published by Dempsey & Windle in 2021, and *Glory Days*, a collaboration with poet Kelly Davis, was also published in 2021, by Grey Hen Press. Kerry was poet in residence at Rydal Mount, Wordsworth's home, in 2023. Loughrigg plays a very big part in her life.

"As a small child I was always in awe of how Loughrigg's moods changed hourly. Sunlight one minute stormy the next, then as if by magic, swallowed altogether in mist. I loved to watch her rising above the village in snow, greening in Spring and the fire of Autumn from our little shop window. We moved to Skelwith from London in 1950, and to make ends meet, my mother opened a bed and breakfast and a tea garden to serve the many walkers passing by.

"Growing up there during the 1950s and 60s was very different from how life is today. All the houses were permanently occupied, we knew everyone, they all worked together to keep the village alive. I remember how mum walked over with her first dog, Kim, to Ambleside most days to do her shopping, it was a stroll to her. She was a keen fell walker and when I was very young, she'd drag me up the bracken slopes.

"It was worth it, and always took my breath away in more ways than one, as the views over to Grasmere, down Windermere, across to Grizedale and toward the Langdale valley and the Pikes felt as though we were at the top of the highest mountain in the world. Our first stop was the seat on the first rise and if we were lucky, we'd watch wild geese flying north or south between scudding clouds. These moments will never leave me, and often appear in my poetry. Loughrigg felt like our fell, our friend, always there to escape to and enjoy. As a teenager my boyfriend at the time, Stephen Darbishire, and I would walk up in evenings for a swim in the tarn, or to simply be alone together. Stephen became my husband in 1967 and being an artist, feels the same as me about this fell and has painted it many times.

"As I write this, I'm looking at my mum's five-year diary, and on this day in March, 1963, she writes: 'Lovely spring day, took Kim over Loughrigg, collected paint from Tinny Martins for the shop, home before rain.' Many things and people come and go but Loughrigg will always be there withstanding the ever-changing skies."

Dr David Cooper is a senior lecturer in English at Manchester Metropolitan University. Much of his undergraduate teaching feeds off, and back into, his research specialisms on post-war/contemporary literature and critical theory, with a particular emphasis on the relationship between writing and place. He also has a secondary, but inextricably interlinked, interest in Romantic poetry. And that's where the Loughrigg connection comes in. David will tell his own story about 'glowworms in abundance'.

It's one of those things where, the more you think about it, the less sure you are that it ever happened. Did I *really* witness it? Did I *actually* walk home one night to see part of Loughrigg lit up? I worked at the Wordsworth Trust for four years and, during that time, Loughrigg was inextricably woven into the fabric of everyday life. On days off, I'd walk over the top to go through to Ambleside. Whenever family came to visit, we'd always go for a little stroll along the Terrace. On warm summer evenings, we'd gather on the beach at the foot of the fell to hatch plans for staying in this place forever whilst knowing that, in reality, very few of us would be able to make that happen.

Most Sunday nights, some of us would head over to Elterwater for the quiz at the Britannia Inn. If it was chucking it down, then we'd all cram into my Nissan Micra. More often than not, though, we'd walk from Town End, around the lake, and over Red Bank. I can't remember why but, one summer evening, I left the pub early and walked back home on my own. When I'd first moved up to Grasmere I was amazed by the night sky as, for the first time in my life, I realised that the Milky Way was the stuff of matter rather than myth. At the time, I didn't really think about the privilege of feeling safe and secure enough to wander around alone in the dark; but solo night-walks in and around the valley were part of my routines and rituals as I began to map the stars.

That night, however, my eyes were involuntarily drawn just a little way up the fell rather than towards the sky. As I walked along the Terrace, and looked to my right, a section of the bracken was illuminated by a constellation of little lights. There weren't scores of them; but there were enough for me to notice and to wonder if I'd happened upon an impromptu installation by one of our artists-in-residence. As I dropped down towards the footbridge, those little lights began to fade from view. Yet I was sure that they were still out there.

"Did you see them? Those tiny little lights on Loughrigg?"

The next day, my questions were met with derision.

"No, we didn't, David."

"Don't you think that it's odd that nobody saw them but you?"

"Just how many did you have last night?"

Later that day, it was my turn to lead timed tours of Dove Cottage. Whilst waiting for the next group to congregate, I started flicking through the copy of Dorothy Wordsworth's *Journals* that was always left in a cupboard in the house. One entry, dated Wednesday, 8 October 1800, immediately caught my eye:

'We walked a very mild moonlight night. Glowworms everywhere.'

Back in my room that evening, I found more references in Dorothy's text:

'Glowworms in abundance.'

' [...] about 6 glow-worms shining faintly.'

'Walked on the White Moss – glow-worms.'

Again, though, I started wonder about it all. Since arriving in Grasmere, I'd found myself more and more interested in Dorothy Wordsworth: a writer who, up until then, had been nothing more than an editorial footnote in anthologies of Romantic poetry. I read fragments of the *Journals* during working hours and, in the evenings, I re-visited passages whilst waiting for the others to get ready to head down to Tweedie's. (The locals' bar in Grasmere). I became obsessed with her remarkable ability to notice and to note. Maybe my friends were right, then. Perhaps I *had* imagined it all. But Dorothy's *Journals*, rather than the pints of Cumberland, were to blame.

I'd completely forgotten about all of this until, last year, I spotted a cluster of tiny little lights as I looked through my reflection on the daily commute back from Manchester. I don't know what those lights were but, at the end of another long day, they instantly transported me from the overpacked and overheated train carriage to that night, twenty years earlier, walking along the Terrace. I guess that there's a good chance that, looking back now, I might be misremembering everything: the post-pub encounter; the conversations at work; the obsessive reading of Dorothy's *Journals*; and even the more recent train journey back home. My story, though, is that, one night, I was lucky enough to see 'glowworms in abundance' on Loughrigg and I'm sticking to it.

And so to the story of the raven, but there's much more first that Julie Coldwell wants to say about Loughrigg. She's a writer and adventurer. She thinks nothing of packing a couple of panniers and cycling round Scotland, or Finland, and wild camping is her idea of a great night out. It seems important that she should have the last words here, because her relationship with Loughrigg is the most intimate.

It was a race against nature to arrive before the impending sunset; I huffed and puffed up the last hill section, raced across the rough stubble and reached the deserted tarn just as the low clouds hovering over the far fells began to glow a faint straw yellow. The harsh caw of ravens echoed in the distance as the brown ducks flapped noisily away to their roost. The living world was preparing for sleep. Time was short for setting up camp before the light show developed. I quickly padded around the perimeter of the water, admiring the glimmering ivy-green reflections of the gentle landscape. Close to the tarn's edge, pinked water-lily pads huddled together, perhaps waiting for their mythical frog prince, while nearby bronzed reeds danced as one in the rustling breeze.

Loughrigg Fell is almost on my doorstep and has been a constant uplifting influence in my life; living in Ambleside means even at the end of an early autumn day when daylight hours are short, one can easily reach the tranquil slopes of lower Loughrigg before sundown. The recent dry spell of weather gave another perfect opportunity to spend a night in nature, away from people and urban distractions.

I could already feel the beginnings of a rising inner calm as I passed through the lichen-covered boulders to a flat grassy area, surrounded by a lofty wall of verdant-green ferns providing shelter from the wind and, importantly, privacy from any passing walkers. It took another ten minutes to establish a cosy nest; the water bottle and flask lie together in the grass; the head torch, phone and specs are carefully placed inside the bivvy bag. Nowadays, I also use an inflatable pillow, which is surprisingly comfortable. Still, my favourite brushed cotton pillowcase always comes along. A homely pillowcase is critical for a good night's sleep.

Abruptly, the pastel light over Loughrigg's summit and the Langdale Pikes is transformed. I snuggled down to enjoy the promise of a spectacular scene to come and wasn't disappointed. The sky began to flush; first came the pale pinks, the clouds' undersides turned burnt orange and flame red, set on a background of streaked aqua blue. The water shone, alight with fiery red-rose reflections, its oval outline flanked by spindly black grasses. The fresh twilight scent and the surrounding colours invoked a euphoric feeling that I was wearing the sunset; it was impossible to drag my eyes away from the beautiful panorama. Near midnight, the rich colours faded to a flat grey, and the chilly dark air wrapped around my shoulders; tired and contented, I sank inside the sleeping bag and floated into a deep slumber.

Suddenly, my sleep hypnosis became invaded by the sound of engines. A cacophony of several trail motorbikes nearby? I scrabbled for the head torch. My first thoughts were: where are those bikes? Are they coming this way? I'm too close to the track. Sitting upright cleared the brain fog, and relief overtook the fear. Feeling rather sheepish, I recognised that the pandemonium was overhead. A low-flying aircraft flew over, followed closely by a helicopter bearing a bright orb of light. It was slightly scary to be awakened in such a manner, and my rapidly beating heart took a while to settle. I lay back and gazed at the now silent expanse of night sky absorbing the twinkling Venus and the millions of tiny glowing stars. Over in the west, high above the inked-out fells hung a delicate sliver of new moon. A blissful sigh slipped from my lips; only an open-air bivvy on Loughrigg could provide such pleasure.

The remote stars were a hypnotic reminder of many nights spent under the radiant skies of New Zealand; always guaranteed to be luminous and dazzling. Engrossed in thoughts of wonder and awe, I scanned the ancient silver river of the mysterious Milky Way when, suddenly, a glowing yellow hub with a brilliant red-orange flared tail hurled itself from left to right across the lower sky. I sat bolt upright in excitement, glued to its brief pathway until it finally disappeared behind the south-facing ridge line. Wow! Was that a fireball? Or a meteor?

Google confirmed it *was* a fireball. Most people are asleep when fireballs can be seen. The daylight typically obscures them from view, and I certainly would have missed this spectacular sighting if not for the noisy night aviators.

The rest of the night passed by without incident. The shadows of dark receded, and breathing in the meditative morning air under a lukewarm sun was a wonderful welcome back into the living world. A band of chattering mallards had already returned to forage on the tarn. The surrounding dew-drenched ferns and pale blue sky outlined the distant Fairfield Horseshoe ridge, a gift from nature and preferable to the village cacophony of delivery vehicles and rattling bins. To my astonishment, it was 7.45. Robert Louis Stevenson asserted we should *"throw our clocks and watches over the housetop and remember time and seasons no more"*. Excellent advice: it felt good and freeing to have stepped out of Ambleside time into the harmonic influence of Loughrigg. As fate would have it, a man suddenly appeared on the adjacent path; after exchanging morning greetings and ignoring his quizzical expression, I grabbed my rucksack and skedaddled to the Tarn to converse with the begging ducks. The passer-by disappeared.

As I relaxed on the wobbly waterside bench, an enormous glossy purple Raven perched on a nearby knoll caught my attention, and I wondered if this enigmatic Raven was Colin. Jim, a pensioner friend in Ambleside, has named his Loughrigg Raven pal 'Colin'. Several times a week at dawn, Jim would walk from the village onto the slopes of Loughrigg. Over a couple of years, numerous mornings and the sharing of many loaves of bread, Colin and Jim developed a mutual trust. Eventually, the Raven brought along his special mate and youngsters to meet Jim and, of course, enjoy a dawn feast.

When it was time for Jim to return home to Ambleside, Colin would accompany him for a quarter of a mile until they met a boundary gate, but never any further. Then, three years ago, disaster struck. Jim was admitted to Preston Hospital with organ failure, close to death. He spent more than two months in hospital and when finally released, he could only walk about fifty yards with the aid of a walking stick. But Jim is determined. He worked hard to regain as much walking ability and health as possible to tackle the slopes of Loughrigg once again.

Corvids are known to be an intelligent species; Ravens can recognise faces and carry out intelligence tests. There's no doubt that Colin was in a morning rhythm of meeting Jim, and he would have felt a loss of sorts as Jim himself did. Eventually, after two years of a complex, protracted recovery, Jim managed to step further and further onto the slopes of Loughrigg to the area where he used to greet Colin. Heartbreakingly, Colin the Raven and his clan were nowhere to be seen. But Jim persisted; for months, he continued to rise at dawn, fill his pockets with bread and seeds, and walk onto Loughrigg, hoping that one day the Raven would return. Then, one early spring morning, Colin materialised from who knows where. It was a fantastic reunion for them both. Jim told me that he'd lost hope in meeting the Raven again, and secretly, so had I. Now, regardless of the past, the Raven family continue to enjoy breakfast with Jim. After each morning encounter, Colin walks with Jim to the same wooden gate before returning to his extended family.

Loughrigg Fell can weave her spell over anyone who is respectful and humble in her presence. As Mary Oliver wrote in her poem, *Sleeping in the Forest* (Little Brown 1979):

> *I thought the earth*
> *remembered me, she*
> *took me back so tenderly, arranging*
> *her dark skirts, her pockets*
> *full of lichens and seeds. I slept*

as never before, a stone
on the riverbed, nothing
between me and the white fire of the stars
but my thoughts, and they floated
light as moths among the branches
of the perfect trees. All night
I heard the small kingdoms breathing
around me, the insects, and the birds
who do their work in the darkness. All night
I rose and fell, as if in water, grappling
with a luminous doom. By morning
I had vanished at least a dozen times
into something better.

Mary Oliver (1935-2019) was an American poet who won the Pulitzer Prize. She found inspiration for her work in nature and had a lifelong habit of solitary walks in the wild

Soundtrack: Over the hill, John Martyn

ABOUT THE AUTHOR

Eileen Jones is a journalist and author who lived for 13 years at the foot of Loughrigg Fell in Ambleside in the Lake District and walked or ran to the summit almost every week during that time. She's previously written a biography of Neil Kinnock, and two books about parkrun, she reviews theatre on her Stagey Lady blog, and as Cumbria PR has worked for some of the leading heritage and tourism organisations in the Lakes.